MW00710269

99 BEERS OFF THE WALL

A Crazed Guide and Twisted Travelogue of One Man's Journey to 99 Bars in New York City in Seven Days

99 BEERS OFF THE WALL

A Crazed Guide and Twisted Travelogue of One Man's Journey to 99 Bars in New York City in Seven Days

Marty Wombacher

99 BEERS, LLC

CORNWALL • 2001

DISCLAIMER

Dear Reader, this volume was written by a known inebriate during the course of one week. Due to his alcoholic stupor, various errors might have entered into his careful and curious research. While the publisher has made every effort to scrutinize the author's quite copious notes (on the back of napkins) and to cross reference the most damaging reviews with collateral photographic evidence, we cannot guarantee the total elimination of erors. Further, the author has admitted in the text to many dubious practices, some of which might be considered illegal in various States of our glorious Union. We do not recommend these stunts and hijinks to any reader nor do we wish to confer any nobility to the author's besotted ramblings. But you did opt to buy a book about bars, so unless you are in fact Carrie Nation reborn for our blessings in this new millennium, then just fuck off. On second thought, even if you are Carrie Fucking Nation, go fuck off anyway. Your ideas about banning liquor didn't work any better than Lenin's brave new order or for that matter George W. Bush's third grade teacher telling him that he'd never get ahead without diligent work. Oh yeah, there's one more thing: some bars might have actually tried to clean up so they could try and sue us. We want them to know that we've got pictures, and unless they want to have the Judge take a whizz in their filthy john, then maybe they should just be quiet and hope nobody reads this damn book anyway.

Cover & Book Design - Joe Freedman
Copy Editor - Jonathan Lesser

Copyright © 2002 by Marty Wombacher
Published by 99 Beers, LLC, P.O. Box 12, Cornwall, CT 06753
ISBN 0-9716386-0-8
All rights reserved. No part of this book may be reproduced or transmitted in any form or by any means, electronic, mechanical, photocopying, recording, or otherwise, without the prior written permission of the publisher.
Printed in U.S.A.

For more information regarding permissions please contact us at info@99beersoffthewall.com

WWW.99BEERSOFFTHEWALL.COM

DEDICATED TO PHIL

the bartender at the Tip Top Tavern

who served me my first beer in a bar

when I was 16 years old.

AND TO MY MOM AND DAD

who helped clean up the puke

off the bedroom floor that night.

"Oh boy, look at all the beer we got!"
—*Curly in the Three Stooges short*
Beer Barrel Polecats *(1946)*

CRACK WHORES

SMELLS OF ASS

GUYS PLAYING WITH THEIR BALLS

PEOPLE WITH PEZ COLLECTIONS AT HOME

OLD GEEZERS HOPPED UP ON VIAGRA

CONAN O'BRIEN

FABULOUS BABE BARTENDERS

PATRONS UNFAMILIAR WITH THE ART OF SELF-DEODERIZATION

MAJORITY OF PATRONS ARE LIFETIME MEMBERS IN THE JUDY GARLAND FAN CLUB

FREE FOOD

BATHROOMS THAT COULD DOUBLE AS HUMAN WASTE MUSEUMS

STEVE DUNLEAVY

PEOPLE WHO LIST "SCAB PICKING" AS A HOBBY

TOURIST FREE ZONE

TOURIST CROSSING

MEN WEARING SUSPENDERS WHO AREN'T EMBARRASSED THAT THEY'RE WEARING SUSPENDERS

FUTURE *MAXIM* INTERNS

I SEE DEAD PEOPLE

AND STARRING JERRY MATHERS AS THE BEAVER

CHEAP BOOZE

CONTENTS

Acknowledgments	9
Introduction	11
Sunday	17
Monday	39
Tuesday	58
Wednesday	79
Thursday	99
Friday	126
Saturday	147
Afterword	163
Bar List by Location	166
Bar List by Quality	170
Index	172

ACKNOWLEDGMENTS

Thank You: Anne & Gerry Wombacher, Terry, Tom & Jim Wombacher/www.swamistuff.com and their various husbands, wives, cats, dogs, rats and birds, Eugenia Kowalski, Frank Chang and Lulu!, Alex Totino, Wendy Gabriel, gob.vision, Lois Marino, Wendy Wynns, Frank Scott, Dick Stolley, Bob Guccione Jr., Jane Pratt, Wes Smith, Russ Smith, *NY Press*, Mike Neill, Bill Bell, Josh Dean, Tim Hennessey—the spiritual guru, Joe Angio, *Time Out New York*, Mike O'Connell, all the poor souls who work with me at my night job, all the poor souls who worked with me at my night job and have been laid off, David "Amigo" Santiago—the unofficial spokesman for Budweiser, Ellen Sugarman, Tracie Hoyt, Tom Lupoff, Hap Mansfield, Lemon and everybody at www.toastmag.com, Brad Elvis, Chloe F. Orwell, www.bighello.net, David Deak, Karen Hudes, ny.citysearch.com, John Whitehead, *Gadfly* magazine, www.gadfly.org,

Pam Klaffke, James Mollo, Paul Harpman, everybody from *fish-wrap,* everybody from *POP* magazine and of course everyone in the wart removal business. Koo koo ka choo Mrs. Robinson.

Special Thanks to: Cyndi Stivers at *Time Out New York,* who originally published my "16 Beers in 16 Bars in 16 Hours" piece, which was the genesis for this book, and to Brandon Holley, who was my editor for that aforementioned article.

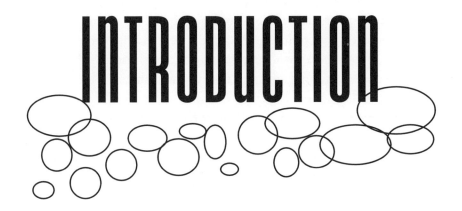

INTRODUCTION

Who died and made Tim and Nina Zagat King and Queen of New York City nightlife? In case you don't know, Tim and Nina Zagat are the couple that produces the Zagat Survey guidebooks. These books are quoted all over the place and are supposedly the top of the line as far as guidebooks go. Well, I recently picked up the Zagat Survey 2001 New York City Nightlife Guide and was appalled to find out that Tim and Nina Zagat don't write most of the reviews. The way it works is they have a card in the front of the book that you can fill out and then be a part of their team of "surveyors." Loosely translated, anyone can write a review for these people and part of it may be quoted in their stinking book!

In this edition, Tim and Nina proudly proclaim that more than 3,200 people participated. Now, they couldn't possibly know all these people or have any clue as to their credibility. Who knows what kind of stone-cold freaks are sending in this information? I mean, let's say Mariah Carey filled out a card in the midst of her nervous breakdown last summer? I'm not making light of Mariah's medical condition, or Mariah herself. I have the utmost respect for this pop diva. She's talented, is blessed with a six-octave vocal range, has giganzo fake breasts and made it to the top the old fashioned way: she married some big fat slob who owned a record company and then divorced his sorry-ass once she was a superduperstar. But let's just say Mariah found one of these books in her hotel room and decided to review some bars. I don't know about you, but I don't want to be drinking in some joint that's recommended by someone in the throngs of a full-blown nervous breakdown. God only knows the places she might recommend. While I've never had a full-tilt nervous breakdown, there was a time about four years ago that I was really stressed out and got a little weird in the head myself. I was kind of freaking out in my tiny apartment and decided to go stand in a Fairway produce market. In case you don't live in New York, Fairway is a produce market and food store on the Upper West Side of Manhattan. And it's always jam-packed with shoppers. Most people who live in Manhattan all say the same thing about Fairway:

YEAH, I KNOW THIS ISN'T A BAR, AND IF YOU'D START READING THE BOOK INSTEAD OF JUST THE CAPTIONS YOU'D KNOW WHY THIS PICTURE IS HERE.

"Love the food, hate the line and the crowd." And I did too, except on this day when I freaked out. I stood in the middle of Fairway and for some insane reason the crowd made me feel safe. I was finally rocked back to sanity a half hour later when some smelly Frenchman hit me with his baguette and told me to "Get out of zee way!" So the point I'm trying to make here is that at that moment in time, I would've recommended to anyone in shouting distance that standing in the middle of a crowded Fairway is one of the most relaxing and enjoyable moments a human being could savor. In truth, Fairway can be one of the most nerve-wracking grocery stores packed with wall to wall people on this planet. The lesson to be learned is this: Don't read guidebooks written by people having nervous breakdowns. That's where I come in.

This guidebook is written by one and only one person, me. And I'm qualified. I've been drinking in bars since I was 16 years old. And I'm a published bar critic. In 1998 I wrote a three-page feature story for *Time Out New York* titled "16 Beers in 16 Bars in 16 Hours." They actually paid me to run around and drink 16 beers in 16 hours at 16 different bars and write a review of each place. So I've got experience when it comes to this bar-review business. I've also gotten paid for writing bar reviews for ny.citysearch.com. I've never seen Tim or Nina Zagat's byline anywhere other than their own self-published books.

And I'm going to tell the truth. There'll be no sugar-coating here. That's something else I noticed about the Zagat's guidebooks, they always try to spin some niceness in their reviews. Here's their review of the Holiday Cocktail Lounge located at 75 St. Marks Place (the surveyors' comments are in quotes): *The best place to go if you lose your job"* this ultra *"cheap"* East Village *"alcoholics paradise"* has a *"terrific,"* *"depressing dive"* atmosphere *(à la the bar in the* Deer Hunter*), with "sticky floors," a "black and white TV," "Christmas lights,"* and an *"old bartender"* who somehow makes *"any drink you order a Budweiser."* So I decided to go and check this place out, and here's what I discovered: It's a perfect example of one of the worst trends popping up these days, the faux dive bar. The faux dive bar is a small bar that's tricked out to look like what the owner imagines is a dive bar, but in reality it's a place for yuppies to hang out and pretend like they're "slumming it." And this joint has faux dive bar written all over it. As you walk in, you discover the bar has two rooms. The one in front has a small dark wooden semicircle bar that's void of any cigarette burns and/or stains. The crowd on this afternoon consisted of a tall black guy jabbering on a cell phone about what time he was going to pick up the groceries, and a white Ken-and-Barbie-doll-like couple discussing the merits of expensive turntables and how it's really nice to be able to afford a car in the city, while the juke-box played Annie Lennox crooning "A Whiter Shade of Pale." The back room is filled with spit-polished brown vinyl booths with nary a tear on the seats and a floor so clean you could eat off of it. The bartender appeared to be in his mid-40's and contrary to the *Zagat's* review, when I ordered a Heineken, I got a green bottle with a Heineken label that didn't resemble a bottle of Budweiser at all. I guess you could call this place a dive bar, because after listening to the yuppie couple blabber on and on about all their possessions, I wanted to dive into my apartment

IS IT THE TOP OF THE MORNING OR THE BOTTOM OF THE EVENING? ONLY HIS BARTENDER KNOWS FOR SURE.

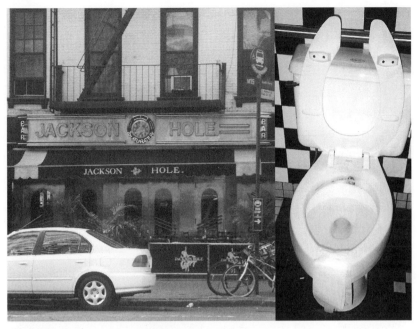

THE TOILET AT JACKSON HOLE. OH TY-D-BOWL MAN, WHY HAVE YOU FORSAKEN US?

and lock the door forever. Golly, I wonder who wrote that *Zagat's* review? Hmmm. . .do you think maybe it was a certain pop diva with a six-octave voice range and giant fake breasts who recently had a total nervous breakdown? Maybe, maybe not. That's the point, you don't know. At least here you know who's dishing out the reviews. Me, me and me. Oh, and one final thought for the *Zagat's* people: The best place to go to after you lose your job is the unemployment office, then you go to the bar. If you people had one shred of street sense you'd know that, but by now we all realize you don't.

Okay, now you may be thinking, "Wait a second, maybe he reviewed that bar correctly, but why should we trust this guy's reviews? After all, he admitted he had some sort of mini-break-down a few years ago." That's a valid point and one I addressed before I started writing this book. I systematically asked four different friends of mine if they thought I was sane, and one by one the answer that consistently flew back was a resounding, "Yes!" Oh, okay, a couple wavered a little, but they came 'round eventually. So there you go. If three out of four dentists are trustworthy, four out of four friends is gold! I'm sane as sane can be, and you have my word that if I start having a nervous breakdown, I'll stop reviewing.

The other question you may have is why 99 bars? Well, in addition to being a pun on the "99 Bottles of Beer on the Wall" song we all tortured our parents with while sitting in the back of the station wagon on summer vacations, it's also Barbara Feldon's name on my one of my all-time favorite TV shows, *Get Smart,* and it was a hit song for one of my least favorite bands, Toto. Besides, do you really need more than 99 bar reviews? I mean, how many bars can you actually hang out in? If it's more than 99 I have four words you may be interested in: The Betty Ford Clinic.

The final question that you, Dear Reader, may have is why cram all 99 bars into seven days? Well, that's because like so many other writers here in New York, I have to work a menial full-time night job in order to afford some of the necessities of life, like rent, pizza and basic cable TV. I only had one week of vacation left at my job, and I decided to use it to run around town and write not only a guidebook, but also a running travelogue of zipping around New York City. Sure, it's going to be a tough job,

I THINK I'M TURNING JAPANESE, I THINK I'M TURNING JAPANESE, I REALLY THINK SO.

but someone's got to tell the truth. Besides, this was the only way of spending my entire vacation hanging out in bars, drinking beer and not having to deal with some sort of intervention at the end of the week.

Cheers!

SUNDAY

SUNDAY

BLOODY SUNDAY

11:30 A.M. Jesus God, it's hotter than Satan's ass out here. I'm walking eastbound on 19th Street heading toward 3rd Avenue. It's already in the 90's and the weather (on the ones) on NY1 said we could break heat records all week long. I'm sweating like a lunatic.

12:05 P.M. I made it to the first bar on my schedule (Paddy Maguire's; I decided to go to Irish bars all day) but the stout Irish woman behind the bar told me to come back at 1:00 when they open. I called the night before and some Irish hooligan told me they opened at noon on Sunday. I've got to stop being so trustful of people. This asshole single-handedly fucked with my schedule and now I'm paying the price for it. He's somewhere in this city having a good old "Irish chuckle" at my expense right at this stinking moment. Oh well, fuck it, I'll walk around and find a diner to get something to eat.

12:10 P.M. I've walked three blocks and can't believe what I'm looking at on the corner of 22nd and 3rd: the Lyric Diner. The fucking Lyric Diner. . .hah! Hah, hah, hah! No, I haven't started drinking yet, it's just that one of my favorite New York stories took place right here in the Lyric Diner.

And here it is: In '97 or '98 a guy we'll call Alvin (I swore to him I'd never tell this story, so the least I can do is change his name) had moved here to Manhattan. He was a writer I had known for a while and we decided to have lunch. He was going to tell me his plans for the future in this city some call the Big Apple. I never do. . .call it the Big Apple that is. I meet him and he suggests we go to his neighborhood diner, the Lyric Diner. So we walk there. It's Sunday around 1:30 p.m., and it's jam-packed with patrons all hungering for a patty melt and fries with gravy and other daily diner specials.

We get a table toward the back in the middle of the rectangular, brightly lit diner. I usually don't eat much in the daytime, so I have a Diet Coke and a glass of water. But Alvin really packs it in. Eggs, sausage, toast, bacon, potatoes, jelly, butter, coffee, and I think cheese was involved somewhere in the course of the meal. It was the brunch special and it was more food than I'd ever seen someone eat for breakfast in my entire life of watching other people eat breakfast. And he was really shoveling it down fast and furious, Fatty Arbuckle style.

He had just jammed the last forkful of the gargantuan feast in his mouth and started to say something, but then he gags. His eyes cross for the briefest of moments, and then he starts choking. I ask him if he's alright and he puts his hand to his mouth. Only one second of normalcy remained for the rest of our stay in the Lyric Diner. For it was then that puke started to stream between his fingers and he stood up over the table and let out an ear-piercing BARRRRRFFFF!! sound and puked all over the table. And then he did it again. And then, just for good measure, he did it once more with feeling.

I AM THE GOD OF HELLFIRE, AND I BRING YOU...BUDWEISER!

By now I've jumped back from the table—which is literally dripping with puke. And we're talking really gross throw-up here, folks, big gray chunks and sickening-looking multicolored runny matter all over our table and dripping down to the floor. By now Alvin has stopped puking and is standing there kind of in a daze. His face is red and his eyes are watering. I look around the diner and it's like someone has shot an Uzi off in the joint. No one is talking, no one is eating, no one is moving. In one instant it went from the typical noisy, clinkity-clank-silverware-hitting-plates diner noise to complete and utter silence.

Everybody is staring at us and the puke-riddled table. It's like time was frozen. And it's at this moment that I see something that I'll never forget. I look a couple of tables ahead of me and off to the left in a booth is a typical Manhattan yuppie power couple with their two boys who look to be roughly five and seven years old. Dad and the boys have on navy blue suits, white shirts and ties and mom is decked out in a summery white dress and wearing jewelry that maybe I'll be able to afford after three lifetimes of working hard labor. The entire family is shiny, clean and polished ten times from Tuesday. And the whole stinking lot of them are staring wide-eyed, open-mouthed at our table that has been turned into a vomitorium. And they all have full plates of food in front of them, they had just been served. I instinctively know that their cherished after-church weekly brunch has been ruined, maybe for the remainder of the summer, perhaps for the rest of their lives. The children would be scarred, that much was certain. But I couldn't waste valuable time worrying about them. I just had to get out of that place and away from the puke.

By this time, Alvin cleans himself up by fouling every napkin at our table. We walk up to our wide-eyed, frozen waitress in the corner and she nervously scribbles out our check. All eyes are glued to us as Alvin places a twenty on her tray and apologizes for the mess she's going to have to clean up. She just stares ice at us. We pay the bill up front to the sickened cashier and as we leave there is still entire silence in the diner. Right at that moment I felt as if I were a member of the Symbionese Liberation Army holding up that bank with Patty Hearst back in the '70s. I hadn't been back to this place since.

And now, four years later, here I am. I have a weird feeling that as I walk in, someone will say, "There he is, one of the throw-up guys. Lynch him!"

1:00 P.M. I made it safely through breakfast (Diet Coke, order of toast, hold the puke) and walked around the neighborhood to kill 17 minutes. It's finally time to duck into the first bar before the sidewalks and street people spontaneously combust into flames from this godawful and terrible heat. I've worked up a powerful thirst. Luckily I've scheduled myself for 17 bars today. Like I always say, "If you can't stand the heat in the kitchen, well. . .you know, just start drinking."

Paddy Maguire's

237 3rd Ave. @ 21st St.

212.473.8407

Beer - Guinness, $5.00

The stout Irish bartender woman is the only person there as I enter the bar. She's reading the Sunday *Times* and barely acknowledges me. I'm in the front room, which has an L-shaped dark wooden bar and stools, all highly polished. The walls are green and white and the usual bar knickknacks are on the walls— beer signs, shamrocks, pictures of horses and the like. Directly across the bar is the jukebox—featuring these Irish classic tunes: "The Juice of the Barley," "A Jug of Rum," and the Irish gay-pride anthem, "The Legion of the Rearguard." And while we're on the subject of rears, in the back room there's two pool tables and a highly polished church pew in the corner. "Bless me father, for I have sinned, it's been two seconds since my last Guinness." So I sit on a stool and order a Guinness. She fills up a glass and barely looks at me as she takes the five. I flip her an extra dollar and say, "That's for you." She barely grunts out a thank-you and goes back to her paper.

THAT TAXI REALLY ISN'T MOVING THAT FAST, IT'S JUST THAT PADDY MAGUIRE'S IS STANDING REAL STILL.

"Hot out today, huh?" I say, trying to get some sort of conversation going.

"Uh, huh," she acknowledges, without looking up from the paper.

"You know I'm going to go to 99 bars this week. It's for a book I'm writing," I volunteer, hoping this will tweak her curiosity.

"Hmmm," is all she says, with her eyes still plastered on that fucking newspaper.

First they tell me the wrong opening time and now I'm being grossly ignored. A more paranoid man would be dripping with conspiracy theories by now. Me, I just sip my beer and let the air conditioning dry my sweat-soaked shirt. Then, BOOM! A door flies open and in walks some short, old duffer with one of those red, bulbous booze noses.

"Hello darlin'," he shouts out in a thick Irish accent.

"Eddie," she screams out, nearly bursting my right eardrum.

He sits down a couple of stools from me, crosses his legs sissy-boy style and she serves him a draft. Then they start talking and joking about the heat. All yuks and hee-haws and whoo-hoo's!

"It said on the news that we're going to break records all week," I throw out, hoping to join in on the funfest. And they both just stare at me. Then they go back to their conversation and totally freeze me out. And it's hard to freeze someone out on a day with 1,000% humidity.

I leave praying, wishing and hoping that their potatoes will always be rotten and their Irish whiskey be alcohol-free.

1:30 P.M. My shirt is soon soaked with sweat again as I head toward the East Village on foot. Soon the stinking process will begin. You may be wondering why I'm walking and not taking cabs or subways or buses. Well, cabs cost money and the subways are void of breathable oxygen on a day like this due to the lack of available fresh air down below street level. Plus, no matter the temperature, subways always stink of urine and other sundry smells in the summertime. And buses, well, they just confuse me. They all run on wacky-ass, zig-zag schedules around the city. First you're going uptown, but no, now we're headed cross town.

But don't get comfortable and don't step over the line, because now we're in the freakin' Bronx. No, buses are the land of confusion, and I have to confess, I've never been a Genesis fan, so today I walk. Sorry Phil, sorry Mike and Tony. . .my God, man, I am so very sorry!

BLARNEY COVE

510 E. 14TH ST. BETWEEN AVES. A & B

212.473.9284

BEER - BUDWEISER, $2.50

This place—dump, if you will—is about as big as three tiny closets and has an unfinished, hooch-stained, cigarette-burnt, old wooden bar running the length of the joint. The walls are a crumbling combo of brick and unfinished wood planks, and it's packed with old, alcoholic men. Some are toothless, others are not. The bartender is a middle-aged woman who looks like she's been around the block more times than anyone would care to know. She has jet-black dyed hair, and arms with old-woman blubber flapping from them. It smells of that weird mothball, old man alcoholic B.O. smell mixed with the aroma of stale beer spilled on the floor that hasn't been cleaned up in decades.

A REAL LOW-RENT RENDEZVOUS.

It's mainly old white/gray guys, but two slightly younger fiftyish black fellows are at the back of the bar. One is passed out and the other just stares straight ahead keeping a tight workingman's grip on his draft beer. Here's a sampling of some of the witty banter that can be soaked in as you drink your beer in this standing vessel of filth and stink: "Fucking faggots are all over this fucking city!" "It's those goddamned Chinese I tell ya, the goddamned Chinamen!" "Fuck the Yankees!" Happily, no one talked to me here, either.

2:30 P.M. I'm taking a much deserved break in Stuyvesant Park between 16th and 17th Streets. It's a small park and there's only one other person within spitting distance, and that's a homeless guy sleeping on a bench with a torn-up cardboard box laying over him. He seems content, so I leave him be. There's an old wooden bench in the shade. I sit down and scan the *Daily News* and the *Post*. Some of the top stories of the day: "Teacher Convicted of Kid Sex," "Madonna Mangles Traffic," "Rehab Lifestyles of the Rich and Famous," and my personal favorite on this blinding hot sunny Sunday: "Granny Dies in Hayride Tragedy." No word on whether Jethro pulled through.

McCARTHY'S

345 2ND AVE. @ 20TH ST.

212.477.6201

BEER - ROLLING ROCK, $4.00

Pretty much your standard cookie-cutter Irish bar. Wooden L-shaped bar, green and dark paneled walls and tables off to the side, blah, blah, blah. Blah-dee-daa-dee-blah. The crowd is

sparse. There's a thirtysomething-year-old tough-looking brunette woman alternately drinking her beer and doing the *Times* crossword puzzle. The bartender is an affable Irish fellow who serves me up a cold Rolling Rock. There's a derelict-looking geezer at the end of the bar drinking a draft and throwing darts with amazing accuracy for someone who looks like a

HELLO McCARTHY'S, HELLO WALLS, HELLO DISEASED LIVER.

cross between a drunken Popeye and an geriatric version of Mickey "Barfly" O'Rourke. Six TV's are all tuned to different channels, and a perky blonde comes bounding in and runs behind the bar. The bartender swats her on the ass and she says in a thick Irish accent, "Be careful there, I might just like that!"

I spend the rest of my stay there engrossed in a private fantasy involving myself, the blonde, a ping-pong paddle and a bowl of Lucky Charms. Take it from me, you don't want to know the specifics.

3:06 P.M. I'm officially starting to stink now.

McSwiggans

393 2nd Ave @ 20th St.

212.725.8740

Beer - Budweiser, $3.00

McSwiggans Bar
393 Second Ave.
(Bet. 22nd & 23rd St.)
New York City

Another Irish bar with no surprises. Dark wooden bar, crowd consisting of middle-aged neighborhood locals, three TV's, a jukebox, a backroom with tables and a pool table, and one portly Roseanne-type looking woman who smiles at me. Story of my life—I fantasize about the blonde and a bowl of Lucky Charms and I get Roseanne and a bottle of Bud.

4:00 P.M. Heading toward 3rd Avenue a couple of minutes ago a most unusual thing happened to me. I tripped a cripple. It sounds almost like a Jerry Springer topic, "Today on Springer—beer drinkers who trip cripples!" But just like NRBQ once sang, "It was an accident." There was this guy who looked like Freddy Fender and he was on crutches but had them stuck out at the sides while walking in a sort of flailing motion. It's hard to explain, but as I was passing him somehow my left foot got tangled in his right crutch and he went flying backward. He was cursing in Spanish at me as I helped him up, and everybody on the street was staring at me like I did it on purpose or something.

That I didn't get, I mean, who trips a cripple? Oh, okay, I did. But it's not like I planned it, so quit looking at me! At least he wasn't hurt. He continued cursing as he hopped away. I feel like the anti-Jerry Lewis. . .or something. Yes, definitely something.

McCORMACK'S

365 3RD AVE. BETWEEN 26TH AND 27TH STS.

212.683.7027

BEER - CORONA, $4.50

This tavern/restaurant is a little more on the high end of the Irish Bar food chain. The place is divided into two sections, a bar room up front with a long, 20-foot bar and dark wood paneling and two TV's, and a restaurant in the back. It's a bit of a fancy-ass place, and two tourists at the end of the bar staring at a giant map. A few other locals are nursing their beers and complaining about the heat outside. Everything looks new in the place, and as I take my notes the bartender, who resembles a young Mel

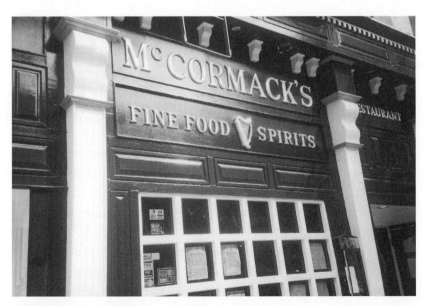

THE NAME: McCORMACK'S. THE FOOD: FINE!

Gibson, notices me writing and wants to know if I'm writing a book.

"As a matter of fact I am," I tell him, and then I explain my 99-beers-in-99-bars mission.

"They did something like that in *Time Out New York* magazine a couple of years ago," he tells me. I explain to him that I wrote that article, and all of the sudden I'm a celebrity in the joint. Mel's telling me Irish bars I have to include, some of the regulars are chiming in with suggestions, everybody's telling me their name and how to spell it and I'm longing to be back at Paddy Maguire's where nobody would speak to me.

4:40 P.M. Things are looking up. The streets aren't as crowded as usual, and I haven't tripped a cripple in over 40 minutes. It could be the luck of the Irish, but more than likely it's the fact that it's so hot out most sane people are home sitting close to their air-conditioning window units.

PADDY REILLY'S

519 2ND AVE. @ 29TH ST.

212.686.1210

BEER - HARP, $4.00

As I sit in this home-styled, kitchen-cabinets-on-white-walls tavern, I'm pondering one question: Who in their right mind names their child Paddy? How does that happen? "Honey, let's name him Paddy. . .and destroy his life!" Oh, and there's a jam session happening in the room off to the side of the bar. Neighborhood people carrying guitars, banjos, mandolins and fiddles wander in and start playing along. Oh, and it's not very good.

PADDY REILLY'S MUSIC BAR
LIVE MUSIC EVERY NITE

BE SAFE ☺ KEEP COVER CLOSED

5:15 P.M. Did I mention I'm starting to stink?

BLARNEY ROCK

137 W. 33RD ST. BETWEEN 6TH AND 7TH AVES.

212.947.0826

BEER - BUDWEISER, $3.75

A wooden leprechaun situated outside of this bar announces that there's "14 TV's inside!" The old-world ancestors of the people who own this joint must be *so* proud! This is a big, honking, no-frills bar with old Kool-Aid-stand type tables, peeling vinyl chairs and a huge bar running the entire length of this dive. It kind of resembles one of those old automat diner places that used to be in Times Square. The crowd is a woozy-boozy mix of tourists all looking to whoop it up in the big city and regulars who have probably paid for their bar stool 112 times over. You can spot the regulars, they're the ones who appear to be ten seconds from falling face-first into their booze. Ray, the bartender on duty, is a friendly Irish guy who informs me that you see *all* the wackos in here. So if you're in a wacko-watching kind of mood, this is your place. If not, well, that's not my problem, now is it?

GONE TO PEE

LEAVE MY DRINK ALONE

BLARNEY ROCK PUB

137 WEST 33RD STREET • NEW YORK, NY 10001

THIS SIGN BROUGHT TO YOU BY THOSE HILARIOUS PEOPLE WHO MARKETED THE "THIMK" POSTER.

5:50 P.M. I'm starting to get a little loaded, so I've decided to stop off at Nathan's Famous Hot Dogs across from Penn Station and get something to eat and take a break. I've got to pace myself. I'm not even halfway through the day's list of bars. Slow and steady wins the race. But then I'm not in a race, so what the hell.

6:00 P.M. Here's a math equation I just learned the hard way: 7 beers + 3 hot-dogs eaten in 5 minutes = massive heartburn. I make a Tums stop at a nearby deli.

BLARNEY STONE (THREE LOCATIONS)

106 W. 32ND ST. BETWEEN 6TH AND 7TH AVES.

212.502.5139

410 8TH AVE. BETWEEN 30TH AND 31ST STS.

212.997.9248

340 9TH AVE. BETWEEN 29TH AND 30TH STS.

212.502.4656

BEER - BUDWEISER AT EACH ONE, $3.00

I've decided to review all three of these places at once, because they're basically all the same bar/hole in the wall. Grumpy old codgers are on both sides of the bar in a dumpy old-time-tavern setting with the baseball game blaring on the TV. I'm keeping the review short because the Blarney on 8th Avenue brings back another favorite New York story of mine—don't worry, this one doesn't involve puke.

It was in the fall of 1995 and I was hanging out in midtown with my best friend, Eugenia. We were trying to find a bar on a Sunday night and we were in one of those parts of town where there's just no bars. We finally find a French restaurant some-where around 30th Street and 7th Avenue that had a bar in the front. We walk in and right away we get snooty-ass, nose-tilted-upward-like-there's-a-bucket-of-shit-under-their-chins looks from the stuffy crowd inside. It was an older suit-and-tie crowd and we definitely didn't look like we fit in there. I'm decked out in my usual 12-year-old, beaten-up black leather motorcycle jacket, ratty black jeans and an overall disheveled, guttersnipe appearance. Eugenia has on tight black vinyl pants, a leopard pat-terned top, pink scarf and black leather jacket. She's also tower-ing over me in black boots with six-inch heels. We kind of resem-

THIS GREAT INSTITUTION STAYED OPEN DURING RENOVATIONS.
TOO BAD.

ble Sonny and Cher gone woefully awry. The patrons don't appear to be particularly thrilled to have us in the place, even if we are just going to the bar. And speaking of the bar, the bartender was a complete and utter. . .let's see, how shall I put this?. . .asshole. He defined the words "empty tip jar." We no sooner sit down than he's throwing rude pick-up lines at Eugenia. She's not interested and subtly tries to let the guy know that she thinks he's a creep. Oh, and by the way, Eugenia's subtle hint to the guy was to say, "You're a creep." But this idiot thinks she's kidding. We tell him we're only here for the beer and he dutifully tells us that they serve this wonderful French cream ale. "But," he tells us in condescending tones, "it's a little pricey at $8.00 a bottle."

Like we couldn't afford $8.00 a bottle. Well, actually we couldn't. Four dollars would've been a stretch, but we're not about to let this clown have the last laugh so we order up two bottles and tell the jerk-off to run us up a tab. And this guy is just stupid enough to do it. So, eight bottles later we order another round and the bartender is starting to look at us with a little suspicion because our bar tab is higher than Robert Downey Jr. out on bail.

I'm starting to get a little nervous; I've got about $30 on me and Eugenia has less, meaning the tab already surpasses our gross combined coinage, but Eugenia tells me not to worry, she's got a plan.

And this is her plan: Five minutes later, when the bartender takes a bottle of wine to a table at the end of the restaurant, Eugenia pokes me in the ribs and says, "Let's go!" We make a mad dash for the door and knock over two bar stools in the process. They hit the ground with a resounding *thud, thud* and a *bang.* Everybody in the place is staring at us as we do our "drink and dash" routine. Eugenia high-tails it toward the door and I follow, but bad luck is only steps away. As I run out the door my bag catches on the outside door handle and spills out on the sidewalk with my camera, some papers I needed and my cigarettes flying every which way and loose. We scoop the stuff up and tear down the street. By now the bartender is chasing us, trying to recover his $80 bar tab. He's gaining on us as we turn the corner at 29th Street.

Now, what happens next sounds like something out of a movie, but I swear it's true. Just as we turn the corner a cab is sitting there. We jump in and scream, "Go!" The cabbie asks in broken English, "But where?" "Just go!" we scream in unison and he takes off the instant the bartender is almost in reach of the door handle on the cab. We howl and howl some more as the cab lunges into traffic. The bartender gets smaller in the back window as he screams obscenities and shakes his fist at us. We tell the driver to stop at the first bar he sees and it's the Blarney Stone on 8th Avenue. We run in and drink $3.00 Budweisers while laughing like hyenas on mushrooms at the whole experience.

And I'm laughing again as I finish this beer seated in the same bar stool, years later, once again well on my way to schnockerdom.

Memories. . .la da da da da da daaa.

7:45 P.M. As I make my way back toward 6th Avenue, I pause as I spy a gentleman near Madsion Square Garden who has set up an aluminum folding table on the street and is selling socks.

Nothing else—no books, no bootleg CD's, no incense, no wallets, no T-shirts. . .just socks. Piles and piles of socks. Socks, socks and more socks. White socks, dark socks, women's socks, men's socks, plaid socks, striped socks, polka-dot socks, ribbed socks, thin socks, thick socks, woolen socks. . .what I'm trying to say here is that this fellow has a lot of socks for sale and I sincerely hope that I am making this fact clear to you, Dear Reader. The sock salesman appears to be of Pakistani descent, stands about 5-foot-4-inches in height, and I don't know why, but for some reason I think he has a wonderful sense of dental hygiene. He has that unmistakable look of someone who carries dental floss at all times. And as I'm standing here watching him mind his little portable sock store, I'm wondering. I wonder how much money he makes per day. I wonder if he lives in the city and if he can pay his rent by selling socks on the street outside of Madison Square Garden. I wonder if his dental floss is waxed or unwaxed. I wonder if he wears boxers or briefs. . .or, and excuse me for being so ribald, if he goes "Indian" in this steaming heat and has no underwear on at all. I wonder if he ever drops down on his knees while squealing at the moon like a piglet in heat and begs God for mercy. I wonder if he has ever stared at water running out of a faucet for so long that he involuntarily lapsed into hallucinations while his eyes crossed and his nasal passages clogged. And as I begin to walk away from the Pakistani sock vendor I wonder, does this poor man, this seller of socks, this foister of footwear, understand that it's not really the heat, it's the humidity? As the mind boggles, I continue my trek.

EAMONN DORAN

136 W. 33RD ST. @ 6TH AVE.

212.967.7676

BEER - 16-OUNCE CAN OF BUDWEISER (FROM A DELI), $1.50

I'm dying to get inside of this place and cool down. Even as the sun begins to set, the pounding heat refuses to lighten the stifling

OH NUTS. I MISSED IT.
YET ANOTHER GRAND OPPORTUNITY SHOT TO HELL.

grip it's put on this city. So imagine the combined feelings of dis-
appointment, bitterness, shame and flat-out hostility I experience
as I see a sign on the window announcing to the hot, the weary
and the thirsty customers making their way to the Eamonn
Doran that the joint is closed due to renovation. "Did that bastard who lied about Paddy Maguire's opening have anything to
do with this?" I think while studying the sign. I trace the words,
"now in renovation" with my right pointing finger, worrying that
that dirty rotten son of a bitch was laughing at me from a nearby
rooftop. I decide not to dwell on it; God only knows what other
tricks that Irish fiend was brewing as I stood there ready to col-
lapse from the heat. I consider finding another place, but decide
it would be a journalistic lie to stray from my list. I buy a tallboy
Budweiser from the Tums deli and drink it in the locked doorway, hiding from the cops and that goddammed Irish hooligan.
Across the street a homeless man sleeps on the sidewalk. I toast
him in silence as my head spins from the heat and from this, my
eleventh beer of the day.

8:32 P.M. I have to get a cab. This fucking heat will not let up
and my shirt and jeans are now almost completely soaked with

my own sweat. I guess it beats being soaked with someone else's sweat, but that's hardly a reason for rejoicing. My head is spinning and it's getting rather difficult to walk. I have a fear that those hot dogs I ate may have been tainted. Of course the 11 beers may factor in slightly, but it's probably the hot dogs. Most definitely the hot dogs.

*(***AUTHOR'S NOTE:*** *Due to possible food poisoning and heat exhaustion, my grip on reality was somewhat lessened at this point. I'm adding this note to prepare the reader for several upcoming slightly shoddy choices in the bars I chose to review, below average travelogue diary writing and behavior that differs from my usual sense of good taste, justice and freedom for all. While the food poisoning/heat exhaustion is what I consider to be the main reason for this horrendous behav-*

ior, I also must lay blame to the cab driver who picked me up on 33rd Street. and drove me to midtown. I didn't mean to, but I accidentally passed out. . .errr. . .napped very briefly in the cab. Instead of gently waking me up and requesting his fare which I would've happily paid along with a handsome tip, this rude and mean cab driver with way too many consonants on his nameplate in the window woke this writer up by poking me with a stick and screaming at the top of his lungs, "Wake up! You pay the fare, you wake up! Pay the fare! Pay

and get out of cab!" I mean, that sort of rude behavior would jar anyone's good senses loose as a goose. That and the food poisoning and the heat exhaustion. Maybe the fact that my total consumption of beer at day's end totaled up to 17 had a bit of a bearing on everything, but mainly it was the food poisoning and the heat exhaustion. And that cabbie. That goddammed cabbie. Anyway, all I can do now is promise this won't happen anywhere else in the book, offer my sincere apologies and use this opportunity to tell you straight-faced that I did NOT have sex with that woman. Thank you. This concludes this author's note and this book will now return to 99 Beers off the Wall.)

8:51 P.M. Fucking cabbie prick. Just because I pass out in his cab he fucking pokes me with a stick like I'm some sort of a fucking leper starting a colony in his back seat. Prick!

THE IRISH PUB

837 7TH AVE. @ 54TH ST.

212.664.9634

BEER - BUDWEISER, $3.50

Fuck the Irish. This bar sucks. I'm sick to death of shamrocks and green. "He says to me," 'Musketeer Gripweed,' "he was a tall chap, some would call him weedy, I did, he said to me, and bear in mind we were some few hundred miles behind enemy lines, he said," 'Green, green, green,' "so I did." Thank you Private Gripweed, you can go back to winning the war now. I'm abandoning my schedule and just having a beer in the closest few bars around here. Fuck it all!

I SWEAR I HAD THE CAMERA POINTED AT THE BAR.

9:20 P.M. I hate midtown. Fuckers keep walking into me and then act like it's my fault. Assholes!

LUNDY BROS

205 W. 50TH BETWEEN 7TH AVE. AND BROADWAY

212.586.0022

BEER - HEINEKEN, $5.00

Jesus, could it be any brighter in here? You need sunglasses just to drink in this fucking joint. And if it was any more sterile, patrons wouldn't be able to have children for years after entering this boring-ass place. Fucking tourist trap!

9:48 P.M. Fuck.

MARTINI'S

810 7TH AVE. @ 53RD ST.

212.767.1717

BEER - BUDWEISER, $4.00

This is a bar that specializes in all different flavors of martinis. And I'm writing a book about drinking beer in bars. I mean, they serve beer here, but it's a fucking martini bar. Jesus Christ, I've got my head up my ass!

10:15 P.M. Fuck.

I SWEAR I HAD MY EYES OPEN WHEN I TOOK THIS PHOTO.

SHERATON HOTEL BAR

811 7TH AVE. @ 52ND ST.
212.581.1000
BEER - HEINEKEN, $5.00

Snacks!

10:35 P.M. I was heading out when I see another bar in the hotel. Oh, hot damn!

HUDSON'S SPORTS BAR

(IN THE SHERATON HOTEL)
811 7TH AVE. @ 52ND ST.
212.581.1000
BEER - HEINEKEN, $5.00

Hah! Talk about killing two birds with one stone—I didn't even have to go out on the street to find my next bar. Sports bars suck.

The only people in here are a couple of cement-heads watching a baseball game and two Russians. Russians! Fucking commie bastards!

11:00 P.M. God it stinks out here. I hope it's not me.

MANHATTAN CHILI CO.

1697 BROADWAY @ 53RD ST.

212.246.6555

BEER - BUDWEISER, $3.50

This place is located right next to the David Letterman show. Dave's not here tonight, but some big fat slob inhaling a bowl of smelly-ass chili is. Tub-of-lard bastard.

11:20 P.M. Fuck.

WAS IT ME OR WAS IT THE CAMERA?

MONDAY

A Smorgasbeer
of Bars

I've had six Advil, three 16-ounce bottles of Diet Mountain Dew and four Camel Lights, and I still feel horrible. My head feels like Buddy Rich's snare drum after a four-hour drum-roll and my mouth tastes like a dirty ashtray that's been marinated in stale beer for 32 hours. My eyes are bloodshot and my sideburns ache.

I've scanned my beer-soaked notes from yesterday and realize that I will fool no one by trying to blame my slightly erratic behavior, somewhat flip reviews and less than adequate travelogue writing at the end of the night on food poisoning, the heat or even that despicable, rat-bastard cabbie who prodded me with a stick. No, it's time for me to admit that by the end of the night I was drunk. Loaded. Plastered. Shitfaced. Pie-eyed. Three sheets to the wind. Blotto. What do you expect? I drank 17 beers in one day. I've got to get to 99 bars in seven days, so yes, some nights I will drink a tad more than I normally would while working on a writing assignment. But I should get credit because I'm not taking any drugs. I mean, I could be smoking crack in an alleyway, mainlining heroin and chugging cough syrup in between going to these bars, but I'm not. Alright? So just get off my stinking back about my drinking! Okay? Because I'm sick to death of your nagging and whining and bitching and bothering! So do us all a favor and just shut the fuck up and go make a sandwich or something!

1:18 P.M. I am *so* very sorry! You bought my book and now I'm screaming at you. I didn't mean it. It's the hangover. I'm in a horrible mood and I took it out on you, the generous, loving and caring reader who paid cash money for this guidebook and travelogue. I don't know what else to do, except to reiterate how *terribly* sorry I am. . .and then start drinking again.

COFFEE SHOP BAR

29 UNION SQUARE WEST @ 16TH ST.

212.243.7967

BEER - RED STRIPE, $5.00

There's a massive, sprawling curlicue wooden bar in the middle of the Coffee Shop Bar with booths off to one side, tables and banquettes for eating lunch and dinner off to the other and another, smaller bar in the back. So the good news is, there's usually a good shot at snaring a seat somewhere. But as we all have realized by now in our sorry-ass lives, when there's good news, very often bad news is waiting in the wings, ready to pounce. Such is the case here. This joint is

WAITER, THERE'S A COFFEE SHOP IN MY BAR.

loaded with attitude, mainly from the pretentious crowd that populates this place—which by the way resembles a coffee shop about as much as a giant, brand new, sparkly, corporate Barnes & Noble bookstore resembles the beaten-up yet charming corner newsstand. The majority of the crowd here is young women who are wannabe models and actresses and sleazy guys in phony Wall Street and agent-type mode. Basically the scene in here is this: The wannabe model is fed a line from the phony agent guy promising a photo shoot here, a screen test there. They go home, have sex, and in the morning when the designer drugs have worn off and they've sobered up, they realize that they're both losers. Good looking losers, but losers all the same. The wannabe model becomes a high priced hooker and the phony agent guy gets lucky the next night by telling some crack whore he can get her an audition for the next edition of *Survivor*. Oh, I saw Susan Sarandon having lunch in here once. She's not here today.

2:10 P.M. Once again, sweat is pouring out of me. It's going to be in the upper 90's again today. I'm surprised with all the beer I drank yesterday that foam isn't spraying out of my pores. As I head toward the 14th Street subway station walking down 6th Avenue there are several table-top vendors selling their wares— bootleg CD's and tapes, sunglasses, T-shirts, jewelry and toy dogs with heads that bobble. But there's not a single sock vendor to be seen. I miss the little Pakistani sock vendor. He sold all kinds of socks. White socks, dark socks, women's socks, men's socks, plaid socks, striped socks, polka-dot socks, ribbed socks, thin socks, thick socks. . .oh, alright, I know we've been through this before. It's just that I miss the little fellow. I wonder if he's selling his socks today. I wonder if he's wearing boxers or briefs or. . .holy Lord, I gotta get a life.

2:20 P.M. I'm down in the bowels of Manhattan that some call the subway system. I like to call it the bowels of Manhattan because it smells like a well-used toilet that's seen nary a cleansing product during its existence. And it's at least 10 degrees hotter down here, making it over 100 degrees in temperature. It's like standing in the middle of a sewage steambath in the dark recesses of hell. The only good thing about subways is the vast potpourri of people to watch. On this day you've got your standard New York City patent-pending cup-shaking homeless guy looking for spare change; a fat woman screaming at her two screaming, bratty children to stop screaming; four teenage boys with pants big and baggy enough to house a small off-Broadway production; a couple of business guys loosening their ties as rings of sweat appear on the armpits of their navy blue suitcoats—which appear to have been purchased at J.C. Penney, but don't quote me on that as I'm not completely positive; and two girls who can't be more than 14-years-old who are giggling with each other. One of the girls is wearing a tight-fitting pink half-shirt emblazoned with the words "Porn Star" on it. Her parents must be *so* terribly proud!

2:45 P.M. Thoughts while riding a crammed-to-the-gills subway car from 14th Street to 72nd Street: "Somebody's got their hand on my ass, I hope it's a woman. . .God it stinks in here. . .white socks, dark socks, women's socks, men's socks, plaid socks, striped socks, polka-dot socks, ribbed socks. . .motherfucker! I gotta quit obsessing about that stupid-ass sock guy and his stand. . .maybe I should see a therapist or something. . .my ass itches, but there's no way I'm going to try and scratch it, if that is a guy's hand, I don't want him to think I'm trying to get chummy with him or something. . .I wish that "Porn Star" T-shirt girl was 18. . .I think I'll have something with cheese on it for dinner."

DRIP

489 AMSTERDAM AVE. BETWEEN 83RD & 84TH STS.

212.875.1032

BEER - RED STRIPE, $4.00

Imagine Pee Wee's Playhouse stocked with booze and personal ads and you've got Drip. While this place serves beer and drinks, it's not really your standard bar. The place is loaded with comfortable chairs, couches, coffee and end tables and kitschy bric-a-brac—Cap'n Crunch boxes and Yoo Hoo bottles—all over the walls. In the back there's a big-screen TV, another couch, a coffee table and more chairs. In addition to booze, Drip also serves coffee, tea and assorted pastries. The big hook at Drip is you can pick someone up without having to talk to anyone and no, you don't need to know sign language. While sipping on the beverage of your choice you can flip through books that are filled with personal ads from patrons of Drip. If you want to respond, you take the code from the ad, write a note and give it to the manager.

ANYBODY ELSE HAVE THE WORDS, *DEPENDS DIAPERS* FLASHING THROUGH THEIR BRAINS RIGHT NOW?

Then the manager relays your message to the person who took out the ad, and if the person wants to meet you, a time is set up to meet at Drip. The first ad I read is from a comedic actress who writes in her personal description, "Mental health always rears its ugly head with me." I decide not to respond and make a mental note to pick up the latest copy of *Juggs* later on in the evening.

P&G TAVERN

279 AMSTERDAM AVE. @ 73RD ST.

212.874.8568

BEER - BUDWEISER, $3.50

I love the P&G Tavern. It's your standard straight-up, no frills neighborhood bar, filled with drunken locals who sit and stagger at the wooden bar. The vintage neon sign outside has been used as a backdrop in the movie *Donnie Brasco* and in an episode of *Seinfeld*. This bar has been a fixture on the Upper West Side since 1940. I was a fixture in the bar myself, when I lived in this neighborhood years ago. My favorite P&G story happened about a year after I had moved from the neighborhood. I hadn't been in the bar since I relocated downtown and I found myself on the Upper West Side one night. Since I hadn't been in the joint for over a year, I thought I would stop in and have a beer for old times sake. I walked in, saw the same bartender who used to serve me, but thought he'd never remember me. As I took a bar stool next to a drooling seventysomething-year-old woman, he sees me and shouts out: "Hey buddy, how you doing? I haven't seen you in here in a couple of weeks." Time moves on, except apparently at the P&G Tavern. And that's what makes it so great.

4:00 P.M. I'm standing on the corner of 73rd and Amsterdam and remembering that this is the corner of my first celebrity sighting when I moved to New York in 1993. I remember walking down the sidewalk toward the corner and there were a lot of people out that day, so the sidewalk was crowded. I'm in the middle of this massive moving crowd walking down the street when all of a sudden I hear some sort of loud buzzing noise and people yelling things like, "Hey asshole, get off the sidewalk with that thing." I'm wondering what's going on when the crowd reluctantly starts to part in the middle to let whatever is making the noise through. And just as a small pathway is parted, here comes actor/former *St. Elsewhere* regular Ed Begley Jr. whizzing through on some sort of bulky, electric, scooter/bike thing. I remember standing there watching him make his way down the sidewalk with the neighborhood people hurling abuse at him and thinking, "My first New York celebrity sighting and it's Ed Begley Jr. . . .what a fucking gyp!" I stood there crestfallen for a full minute, then went to the deli and purchased a *New York Post,* which had one of my favorite *Post* headlines of all time. This was during the whole Tonya Harding/Nancy Kerrigan skating scandal, and in huge type on the *Post* the headline screamed out: "Bodyguard Fingers Tonya." I immediately went home taped it to my kitchen wall and tried unsuccessfully to put the Ed Begley Jr. sighting out of my mind.

ERNIE'S

2150 Broadway between 75th & 76th Sts.

212.496.1588

Beer - Amstel Light, $4.50

Ernie's is a restaurant where there's a circular bar in front. It's your standard restaurant bar in your standard, slightly upscale pasta place with high ceilings. There's one other guy at the bar, eating a sandwich, but I think he works here. He's got on a white shirt and black vest, so I figure he's a waiter. I mean, who wears that sort of outfit unless he's a waiter? A ventriloquist perhaps, but the sloppy way bits of the sandwich are falling out of his mouth proves he doesn't have the proper lip control for ventriloquist duty, so he had to be a waiter. There was just no doubt in my mind.

The bartender is a really good-looking woman with reddish hair pulled up into a ponytail, tight black pants and a low-cut blouse that I was able to peer into as she grabbed the beer out of the cooler down below. As she serves me the beer I hit her with this smooth-operator-like line: "So, how's it going?"

She flirtatiously volleys back by saying, "That'll be $4.50" and then stands as far away from me as is humanly possible. Once again, I make a mental note to pick up the latest copy of *Juggs*.

5:00 P.M. I'm on a crosstown bus heading toward the Upper East Side. I know I said yesterday that I never take buses, but this one, which you can pick up at the corner of 79th and Broadway, is a crosstown bus that actually moves cross town and never veers off course. I'm enjoying the air conditioning and eating from a bag of Party Mix snacks that I picked up at a deli. It's a curious collection of varying types of snack crackers all colored orange, although they vary in hue. The snacks are listed on the side of the bag and they include: Crunchy Cheese Curls, Nacho Tortilla Chips, Pretzel Sticks, Bar-B-Q Corn Chips, Corn Chips and Midgees. I have no idea what a Midgee is. I've had Cheez Waffies and they're a delicious snack item. But a Midgee? I repeat, I have no idea what a Midgee is. And I don't feel good about that at all.

OKIE DOKIE

307 E. 84TH ST. BET 1ST & 2ND AVES.
212.650.9420

I'm standing in front of the address which was listed for the Okie Dokie and it's an apartment building. I know I wrote the address down correctly, but it's an apartment building. I can't help but wonder if eating the Midgee has played some sort of role in this most unfortunate occurrence. I decide to walk and stop at the next bar I run into which is. . .

Jackson Hole

1611 2nd Ave. between 83rd and 84th Sts.

Phone: 212.737.8788

Beer - Corona, $3.50

The curse of the Midgee strikes again! This place isn't really a bar after all. I mean, there's a bar in here, but it's more like a lunch counter. You can get a beer here, but they won't let you smoke. What, are we in California all the sudden? This place is a '50s-styled *Happy Days* kind of diner and there's a kid's birthday party going on in the booths behind the bar. Screaming kids, screaming adults and I can't smoke at the bar. And my beer is warm. I decide to use the bathroom and get the hell out of here. Once in the bathroom I make a very unwanted discovery. The toilet has a very scary stain on the bowl. I decide to piss in the sink and vamoose.

MONDAY

Beekman Bar and Books

889 1st Ave. @ 50th St.

212.980.9314

Beer - Anchor Steam, Free

(compliments of Kevin the bartender)

Paul's Grandad: Would ya look at him? Sittin' there with his hooter scrapin' away at that book!

Ringo: Well, what's the matter with that?

Grandad: Have ya no natural resources? Have they even robbed you of that?

Ringo: You can learn from books.

Grandad: You can, can ya? Baahh! Sheeps heads! Ya can learn more by gettin' out there and livin'.

Ringo: Out where?

Grandad: Out any old where! (*sarcastically*) But not our little Richard. Oh no, when you're not pumpin' them pagan skins, you're tomentin' your eyes with that rubbish!

Ringo: Books are good.

Grandad: Parading's better.

Ringo: Parading?

Grandad: Parading the streets, trailing your cove, boring along. . .living!

Ringo: Well. . .I am living.

Grandad: You? *Living?* When was the last time ya gave a girl a pink-edged daisy? When did ya last embarrass a sheather with your cool appraising stare?

Ringo: You're a bit old for that sort of chat, aren't you?

Grandad: At least I've got a backlog of memories. All you've got is that *book*! That bleedin' book!

6:45 P.M. I'm taking my first overdue break of the day at Bryant Park on 42nd and 6th. The park is filled with lots of homeless people in various stages of sleeping, bumming change and taking the occasional puff on a crack pipe—the pause that refreshes. I'm sharing a bench with a man smoking a horrific smelling cigar. He vaguely resembles Cap'n Crunch. As I sit and refresh myself in this 90-plus degree heat, breathing secondhand stinkorific cigar smoke, I'm pondering what sort of army would allow a man like Crunch to rise to the rank of Captain? How did this guy even make it through basic training? What if they gave a war and no one came. . .except Cap'n Crunch? Armed with only a half gallon of low-fat milk and a teeny-tiny little toy? Dear God, I wish I had the answers, but I must continue my journey.

HOWARD JOHNSON'S: THEY GOT THEIR HO JO WORKIN'. THAT'S WHAT
NRBQ SAYS ANYWAY.

HOWARD JOHNSON'S

1551 BROADWAY @ 46TH ST.

212.354.1445

BEER - BUDWEISER, $3.50

The bar at Howard Johnson's in the heart of Times Square is in
the back of the restaurant. It's a tiny square/horseshoe fake wood-
en bar with about ten stools that surround the circumference.
Two ancient orange signs that proclaim, "Cocktails" hover over
the end of the bar. The only two people at the bar consist of myself and an older, grizzled, peroxide-blonde bartender, whom I
assume voted for Nixon in the '60s. She was probably what
Nixon himself would have called a "real looker" in her day, but
those days haven't been around since *The Saturday Evening Post*
ceased publication. There's a certain overall blankness in her
appearance and demeanor that suggests she's worked here her
whole life and has relished every stinking moment of it. As

opposed to the blank look that's coloring my face due to the fact that I'm on my seventh beer, I'm worn down from two and a half days of hiking around Manhattan in blazing, hellfire heat, and I'm going through mild shock that the words "I might let her blow me" just cruised through my brain as I took my first sip of beer. Aaaaahhhhh!

7:30 P.M. My brain actually said to me, "I might let her blow me!" Aaaaahhhhh!

MONDAY

THE MARRIOTT HOTEL BAR

1535 BROADWAY @ 45TH ST.

212.398.1900

BEER - BUDWEISER, $6.22

I feel defeated, cheated and basically fucked on more than several different levels. The Marriott has a bar on the eighth floor that spins real slowly. And the walls are all glass, so you can drink and look at Times Square as you spin. It's quite exciting to sit and observe all the brightly colored billboards, the Jumbotron, the buildings and the tourists below. This is one of my favorite places to drink a beer in all of New York. But not anymore, Johnny, not anymore. As I walk toward the bar I see the area where it used to be is walled off and there's another bar in front of the walled-off area. It's a round bar, but it doesn't spin. They have free peanuts, but it doesn't spin. There's a couple of fabulous babes behind the bar, but it doesn't spin. Of course, none of the fabulous babes

HARD TIMES AT THE MARRIOTT, BUT THEY STILL GIVE OUT THESE GREAT MATCHES FEATURING THIS DRAWING.

wait on me; some dorko with a handlebar moustache—yes, that's right, a freaking handlebar moustache, I mean did he just come from his barbershop quartet rehearsal or what?—takes my order. When he brings my beer I try to hold my composure and ask him, "So, what's up with the bar that spins?"

"Oh, they're remodeling it," he nonchalantly answers, either unaware, or more than likely, unconcerned that my world is collapsing while his creepy moustache continues to handlebar.

"Oh," I say, once again maintaining composure, "so it's going to reopen?"

"Yep," he answers, in a tone so well suited for someone with a grotesque growth above his upper lip.

I brace myself and lock my knees together as I summon up all the courage in my being and ask the following question: "So, it'll still spin, right?"

"No," he callously spits out as he grabs my money and bolts for the cash register.

I couldn't believe it. I mean, I've been ratfucked before, but this was like I was in some otherworldy dimension. The way he was so nonchalant in his answer. What kind of a human being can just stand there, aware that the Marriott bar will never spin again, and just carry on with his job, happy as a fiddler with a freshly stringed violin. Well, yours truly isn't just going to sit here and let his parade be rained on in such a slap-happy manner. I chugged my beer and left without leaving one cent for a tip. Plus, I ate all the peanuts in the bowl. Take that to your barbershop quartet recital and smoke it. . .fuzznuts.

8:45 P.M. A lesser journalist might throw in his notepad at this point and call it quits. Not me. I'm cut from a stronger cloth, burlap perhaps, although it could be corduroy. I decide to fortify myself with a three-piece original recipe meal at the Kentucky Fried Chicken at 50th and 7th. As I sit and enjoy my meal that's housed in a hideously off-register four-color printed cardboard box, I'm pondering what sort of army would allow a man like Sanders to rise to the rank of Colonel? How did this guy even make it through basic training? What if they gave a war and no one came. . .except Colonel Sanders? Armed with only a bucket of chicken and a side of cole slaw? Dear God, I wish I had the answers, but I must continue my journey.

THE HARD ROCK CAFE

221 W. 57TH ST. BET 7TH AVE. & BROADWAY

212.459.9320

BEER - BUDWEISER, $4.00

Things I see while wandering around the Hard Rock Cafe: A framed poster of Sid Vicious playing bass with the Sex Pistols, Fillmore East posters from the '60s, one of Iggy Pop's old guitars, an Electric Flag concert poster, a bass guitar that used to belong to Jeff Ament from Pearl Jam, a poster of Natalie Merchant, three pictures of Tori Amos in concert, a blown-up framed photo of a grade-school-aged Kurt Cobain with an engraved gold plaque at the bottom that's inscribed "Little Kurt," and tables all packed with loud tourists happily munching on what appear to be sandwiches made out of greasy, grimy gopher meat along with mountain-sized side orders of french-fried potatoes. All the while the painfully dull musical stylings of what I think is the Dave Matthews Band, or one of those bands that sound like the Dave Matthews Band, blares out of the sound system. On the way out, above the giant golden double doors, a sign hangs that reads, "This Is Not Here." If only those words rang true, what a wonderful world this would *truly* be.

THE DARK SIDE OF THE HARD ROCK CAFE.

HARLEY DAVIDSON CAFE

1370 6TH AVE. @ 56TH ST.

212.245.6000

BEER - BUDWEISER, $4.00

See Cafe, Hard Rock.

9:50 P.M. I'm proud of myself. I've paced my drinking much better tonight. I haven't taken a cab and I'm still perfectly fine walking around in heat that once again refuses to let up.

HOOTERS

211 W. 56TH ST. BETWEEN BROADWAY & 7TH AVE.

212.581.5656

BEER - BUDWEISER, $2.70

What sort of man drinks at Hooters? He's a lonely, lonely man. Maybe he's kissed a girl, but probably not. He's a fellow who's afraid to look at the woman in tiny orange shorty shorts with breasts spilling out of a tighty-whitey Hooters tank top if she's within two feet of his table. He'd love to be in a strip bar, ogling a *totally* nude woman, but. . .well, what if the neighbors saw him? The spicy chicken wings give him heart-

burn, but he eats them anyway hoping to fit in. He'd give his right hand. . .oh wait, he's going to need that for later. . .he'd give his right leg to buy the latest issue of *Juggs,* but. . .well, what if the neighbors saw him? So he waits patiently for his yearly *Sports Illustrated* swimsuit issue to hit the newsstands while seated at the bar yearning for the day when wingtips finally come back in style.

10:25 P.M. Fuck it, maybe I didn't pace myself as well as I thought. I'm taking a cab to the next place.

10:30 P.M. I'm in a cab heading to the White Horse Tavern in the village. Naturally, the cabbie's first name on his cab I.D. sticker is Achhhmaadquiz. I've rolled the window down so wind blasts in my face and keeps me awake. Achhhmaadquiz has that sadistic look of a stick poker to the Nth degree.

WHITE HORSE TAVERN

567 HUDSON ST. @ 11TH ST.

212.243.9260

BEER - BUDWEISER, $3.00

This classic, back to the basics, old-school tavern in Greenwich Village is filled with regulars who don't play around with their drinks. In fact, this is the bar where Dylan Thomas supposedly drank himself to death. And as I sit at the bar sipping my 28th beer in less than two days, I feel the spirit of Dylan Thomas well up inside of me. Then again, it might just be gas from the Kentucky Fried Chicken.

11:05 P.M. I've decided to take cabs to the remaining bars. After two days of sweating and drinking at a ridiculous clip, my legs feel like they belong on a Gumby doll. Some tiny Asian guy is driving like a madman and I'm getting a serious contact high from the pot smoke in this cab. He must've just finished a giant spliff before he picked me up, cause it smells like a Grateful Dead concert in here. I'd roll the window down, but why waste second-hand pot smoke. Holy shit, he just about got clipped by a huge black SUV. Breath deeply, breath deeply. Yeah mon!

BONGO

299 10TH AVE. BETWEEN 27TH & 28TH STS.

212.947.3654

BEER - PILSNER URQUELL, $5.00

"Hello, Bongo! He's the one with the short, fat, hairy legs, isn't he?"

11:35 P.M. Sometimes there's just nothing clever to write in these passages. This is one of those times.

LIVE BAIT

14 E. 23RD ST. BETWEEN BROADWAY & MADISON AVES.

212.353.2492

BEER - HEINEKEN, $4.50

The last time I was in this bayou/fishing-motif-styled bar, there was this incredible-looking woman bartending. She's not here tonight. No, tonight I'm being served my beer by a young man, who if he doesn't have the title of "King of the Doofuses" already, I'm sure that honor will be bestowed upon him somewhere in the not too distant future. He has the look and demeanor of a mentally challenged Jethro Bodean combined with a Gomer Pyle-styled wit. There are four other loser-type guys all sitting at the bar

staring straight ahead. One of them is trying to tap his foot to the Allman Brothers song "Ain't Wastin' Time No More." He's failing miserably. I stink and I don't even care. In fact, I stink, therefore I am. Ja!

12:10 A.M. This is another one of those times.

OLIVES (AT W HOTEL)

201 PARK AVE. SOUTH

212.353.8345

BEER - BUDWEISER, $4.50

Olives is located in the trendy W Hotel. So wouldn't it make more sense to call this boring-ass, yuppie/trust-fund-kid watering hole X? Or even Y. No, wait, the perfect name to match the ambiance in here is, of course, Zzzzzzzz.

12:35 One more bar to go. . .one is the loneliest number. . . Harry Nilsson wrote that. . .Three Dog Night sang it. . .I've had 15 beers and I've still got to drink one more at one more bar. . .one is the loneliest number. . .Harry Nilsson wrote that. . . Three Dog Night sang it. . .and the Marriott bar no longer spins. It's a cruel, cruel world. I can't remember who sang that, but I'm sure someone did. Maybe Uncle Joe, who's moving kind of slow. . .at the Junction. . .Petticoat Junction.

BIG BAR

75 E. 7TH ST. BETWEEN 1ST & 2ND AVES.

212.777.6969

BEER - BUDWEISER, $3.50

It's called the Big Bar, but in reality it's a tiny little place with a teeny-tiny bar, and teensy-weensy booths. What trickery. What practical jokery. What tomfoolery. What deception. What a ruse. What a fraud. What humbuggery. What wretchedness. What the hell. Whatever. What?

1:20 A.M. Godammit! I forgot to get that copy of *Juggs*.

TUESDAY

ONE ISN'T THE ONLYEST NUMBER

2:00 P.M. Amazing, there's no hangover. The hangover fairy must've chosen to spare me and decided not to sprinkle me with headache powder and dry-mouth dust. Then again, maybe I'm still drunk from last night.

NY1 weather (weather on the ones) just reported that the temperature today will be a skin-blistering 97 degrees, with a heat index of 105. I have no idea what a heat index is, but I'll throw caution to the wind and take their word for it. Here are some of the helpful hints they gave to be safe when you're walking around in this kind of heat: 1. Wear light-colored clothing—every stitch of clothing I own is black. 2. Don't drink caffeine—I just drank two 16-ounce bottles of Diet Mountain Dew. And the final hint for being

PUB   CAFE

ONE AND ONE
76 East First Street
New York, NY 10009

BE SAFE ○ KEEP COVER CLOSED

safe in the heat is: Don't drink alcohol. I'm heading out the door to drink 13 beers in 13 bars today. Translation: I'm fucked as fucked can be.

2:30 P.M. It's such a pot-boiling hot day today that as I pass a fruit stand on 5th Avenue, I expect the peaches and plums to start exploding—pulp bursting through skin like raw eggs in a microwave oven. They don't, but it's only a matter of time, Charlie, it's only a matter of time. That wicked heat index is zooming in from the horizon and the humidity is making the air feel thicker than overcooked chocolate pudding.

I decide to surrender to the heat and take a cab to the first bar (the One and One), which is located at 1st Avenue and 1st Street. (I'm doing a special theme day on bars with the numeral one in their names. Since the Irish-bar theme day went down in disaster, I thought I'd make it up with another theme day. I feel just like Merv Griffin, sans Arthur Treacher of course.) So I'm standing at the corner of 14th and 5th, index finger pointing up toward heaven and all its creatures, trying to hail a cab. I'm not having much luck finding one because everybody's taking cabs today because of the heat. I'm standing on the corner with sweat pouring out of my frying skin for three minutes when some woman who looks like a cross between Dom Deluise and Carnie Wilson before she got her stomach stapled walks up and puts her stubby little chubby finger in the air trying to hail a cab, right next to me. I couldn't believe it; I mean, that's just not done. I'd been there for at least three minutes, I *owned* that corner. It's the rules. So I turn to her and say, "What are you doing?" And she just gives me a look like I'm some sort of a nut job. Believe me, I know that look. So I say to her, "I've been here for three minutes, this is *my* corner." And again she shoots me the insane-guy look. And now a cab pulls up and she starts to get in it, so I say, "That's my cab." She just shakes her head and climbs in with her massive girth jiggling like jelly in a dress all straining to get through the door. Unbelievable! I could feel the air conditioning streaming out of the cab. So she not only stole my cab, she snares one of the few cabs where the cabbie actually turns the A.C. on. "That was my cab," I yell out as they lurch into traffic and speed away. And then, as if things aren't bad enough, a car-service Town Car sees me yelling at the cab and pulls up. The tinted window rolls down and the Japanese driver is yelling, "Get in."

"I'm going to the corner of 1st Avenue and 1st Street," I tell him through the window. "How much?"

Without batting an eyelash, this wicked son of a bitch spits out, "$20, get in."

"What, 20 bucks, are you fucking nuts? I'm just going to the East Side, not the airport," I retort in a pained manner. My shirt is completely soaked with sweat by now, not that this Japanese scumbag on wheels cares. No, this evil bastard doesn't even *pretend* to care.

"Get in," he says, his voice raising like he's pissed.

"Fuck you, I'm not shelling out 20 bucks, it's like a six-dollar cab ride, tops," I say raising *my* voice and upping the ante.

"You want a ride, you pay," he says, raising my yell and taking it up to a scream.

"Get the fuck out of here," I reply, raising his scream to a full-bore yell.

"Asshole," he yells, calling his hand as he speeds away.

"You're the asshole, you're the asshole," I scream about 10

ONE AND ONE: THEY APPEAR TO BE VERY HAPPY WITH THE NAME THEY CHOSE.

times in a row even though he's long gone. And now I get insane-guy looks from every stinking person on the corner.

"He wanted to charge me 20 bucks," I explain to the people staring at me on the corner. More insane-guy looks are tossed my way as I realize the Town Car is long gone, so they must think I'm talking about some imaginary car-service guy. My stomach sinks as I realize my reputation is completely shot on the corner of 14th and 5th for the moment, and quite likely for the entire day. One more corner in the big city where everybody and their cell-phone-jabbering brother thinks I'm a flipping nut job. It just isn't fair.

"I'm trying to do a service for this city by providing it with a new and refreshing guidebook and I'm looked at like I'm Charlie freaking Manson, wide-eyed with a fresh swastika carved in my forehead. There's no justice, no justice," I mumble to myself as I start hoofing it to the One and One. The sweat pours out as the horrid corner of 14th and 5th shrinks in the distance over my shoulder. I make a mental note not to hail a cab from *that* corner anytime soon. They won't have this journalist to kick around any-more. Goddammed rotten taxi thieves.

ONE AND ONE

76 E. 1ST ST. @ 1ST AVE.
212.260.9950
BEER - CORONA, $5.00

This bar has it all. In fact, instead of a review, let's make a check-list. Is it spacious? Yes. Friendly bartender? Yes. Great, fun crowd? Yes. Best fish and chips in town? Yes. Wonderful music? Yes. Exciting decor? Yes. Do they pour the best Guinness in town? Yes. Is it everything that anyone would want, need and crave in a bar? Yes. Are the bathrooms sparkling clean? Yes. Should you drop whatever you're doing and go directly to the One and One now and spend as much money as you can? Yes. Do I know Terry Dunne, the owner? Yes. Does he owe me a free beer? Yes.

3:15 P.M. As I'm walking up 1st Avenue, I see a disturbing sign outside of a restaurant boasting that they now serve a "Waffle in a Bag." Why would anyone be proud of coming up with the idea of putting a waffle in a bag? Why would anyone even admit that they were *thinking* about putting a waffle in a bag? What kind of weirdness is that? I mean what's next, a muffin in a pencil pouch? Pancakes in a FedEx box? People, please, stop the madness. And just like Edwin Starr, I'll say it again, "STOP THE MADNESS!"

WHY. . .FOR THE LOVE OF GOD, WHY?

119 BAR

119 E. 15TH ST. NEAR UNION SQUARE
212.777.6158
BEER - BUDWEISER, $5.00

TUESDAY

This is a three-railroad-style-roomed bar in Chelsea. As you walk in the front room, you're immediately face to face with a pool table. To the right of the pool table is a door to the middle room, which is windowless and very dark. It's here where the bar is

located, and there are a few tables with a couple of beat-up couches lining the walls. The next room has a window, is bright with the sun streaming in and has tables and comfortable stuffed chairs. I decide that the middle room is the smart room to seat yourself in at this establishment. Aside from the darkness and the bar, there's a cute, dark-haired bartender dressed all in black. As I approach the bar I think about making some sort of Bobsey Twin joke with her, since I too am dressed all in black and have dark hair, but then I'm hit with a quick slap of reality. There's a mirror behind the bar, and as I look at myself in it, I see while I *am* dressed in black, my once dark hair is turning gray, I haven't shaved in three days, the bags under my eyes are getting big enough to house waffles and I stink of sweat and beer. I decide to order a beer and let her make the first move. It must be too hot for hell to freeze over, because I finish my beer and no moves on her part were made. Maybe next time, but probably not. Oh well, this just gives me incentive to work harder at my night job when I go back. Hookers aren't cheap these days.

4:15 P.M. The next stop was supposed to be the 101 bar on the corner of W. 4th Street and 7th Avenue, but it's closed. It must not open up till later. These goddammed theme days always seem like a good idea at the time, but now after being burned by both the cabbie and that vile Japanese Town Car villain and getting blindsided by the "Waffle in a Bag" sign, I've decided to abandon this theme-bar bullshit and just hit random bars. I mean, who puts a waffle in a bag, for God's sake?

HEARTLAND BREWERY

35 UNION SQUARE W. BETWEEN 15TH AND 16TH STS.
212.645.3400
BEER - SUMMERTIME APRICOT ALE, $6.00

The Goo Goo Dolls song "Iris" is playing on the sound system as I stroll into the Heartland Brewery. It's the perfect middle-of-the-road song for this perfectly middle-of-the-road bar, oh, excuse me, "brewery." This place has the prefabricated feel of a chain-type bar and that's even more evident as I see Heartland Brewery T-shirts, shot glasses and beer mugs for sale Hard Rock Cafe-style up by the cash register. I take a seat and soak in the ambience of the Heartland Brewery, which consists of wood-trimmed brick walls with horrible heartland-themed murals containing images of farmlands, horses, wagons and tractors painted in a paint-by-numbers style by an artist who appears to have had trouble counting. The crowd consists of. . .how shall I properly phrase this. . .chowderheads. The jar-headed fellow sitting next to me at the bar has a giant glass of beer and is eating some sort of gray-looking meat product with a strange colorful/stomach-turning side order of what appears to be garbage-disposal glop. And since there are no garbage disposals in New York, they must've had to import it. I'm not ashamed to admit that it frightens me. The bartender is a pretty Latin woman, wearing a belly shirt that exposes a silver bellybutton ring on the aforementioned belly. I'm trying to get her attention, but she's staring straight ahead in a vacant, sleepwalker kind of zombie stare. Finally, after moving to a bar stool directly in front of her and waving my hand in her face, I break the spell. She asks, "What can I get you?" in a monotone voice perfect for someone who appears to have endured a full-frontal lobotomy during her last bathroom break. A sign on the way in announced the up-till-now-unknown fact (for myself at least) that "Everybody Loves Summertime Apricot Ale." So I order one. She delivers the beer, err, "brew," and after one sip I discover that there's at least one person who doesn't love Summertime Apricot Ale. And—surprise—it's me. It tastes like goat piss, not that I know what goat piss tastes like, but now I do. As I choke the last sip down, I notice one of the drink specials on the menu is called a "Shandy." It consists of the unlikely and sickening combination of Cornhusker Lager and Sprite. On the way out the door it dawns on me who would invent a gut-wrenching drink like the Shandy. Weirdness like that could only sprout from the "Waffle in a Bag" guy's twisted and sick mind. And I have to admit, I feel no shame at all as I write this next line: Goddamn his rotten soul to hell's fire!

5:30 P.M. I've walked half a block and I'm stunned at what I see on the corner of Union Square West and 15th Street. It's another tabletop sock vendor. And it's not our Pakistani friend from Sunday, nope, this guy is a black man who appears to be in his late 50's. He's got a graying thicket of hair standing straight up à la Don King and a stocky, no-nonsense build. While the Pakistani man was content to run his tabletop business in a peaceful, Zen-like manner, letting customers come to him, not fretting if passerby chose to ignore his table of woolen wares, this guy is harsh as third-rate whiskey. His sales style is more akin to that of a brutish carnival barker. As I stand here looking at his table a good foot away, our eyes lock and he immediately starts screaming at me.

"You need socks?" He barks at me in the gruffest of all manners. His voice is sandpaper rough and hellfire is blazing in his eyes.

"No, I'm good," I reply with a wave of my hand, trying to imply in a subtle manner that I was no fan of the "hard sell" he's trying to lay on me.

"Come on, everybody needs socks in this heat. Three pair for five dollars!" he screams at me in a tone that's far too excited and wild for someone who's a seller of socks.

I stand there for a good 30 seconds trying to figure out what he meant by, "everybody needs socks in this heat." I mean, it didn't make any good sense as far as I could tell. Don't people take their socks *off* when it's hot out? Sure, it's true *I* have socks on, but that's only due to a slight foot fungus, of which I'll spare the dear reader the grisly details. But wouldn't someone who's business is socks be aware that sales would be slightly off in the middle of this hellish heatwave? One would think so. But not this guy, Oh, no, within seconds he's back barking at me to buy something.

"Three pair for five bucks, come on, I'm giving these things away, what's wrong with you?" he roars at me. And now his tone is not only gruff, it's borderline rude. It's time to let him know I'm not going to take this sort of bullshit anymore.

"Look, I don't want any socks, let it go," I say to him firmly, yet in a calm manner so as not to mirror his rudeness. I start to walk toward the next bar when he hits me with the following bombshell.

"Check out the site sometime, my man, buy online," he bellows out to me while pointing to a sign that's hanging from his sock table.

I stop in my tracks, turn around, and I see a sign that reads, "www.socks.com." Holy freaking shit. This guy has a Web site. In terms of technology, he was leaving our Pakistani friend deep in the dust with his dick in the dirt. I couldn't believe it. How was the Pakistani sock dealer supposed to compete with this? It's like a man selling coffee off a street stand trying to compete with the horrible and evil Starbucks Coffee chain stores. He was fucked five ways beyond Friday. I walk off in the direction of the Old Town Bar feeling bad for the Zen-like Pakistani sock salesman. But I couldn't dwell long on this matter, better just to chuck it in the garbage bin with yesterday's bad news and move along quickly, like a ferret with a well-organized Dayrunner. I can't save the world, God knows I've tried. As selfish as it sounds, I have my own problems to deal with. There was beer to be drunk and a scorching heat index to deal with. Et tu, Mr. Pakistani sock seller, et tu.

OLD TOWN BAR

45 E. 18TH ST. BETWEEN PARK AVE. AND BROADWAY
212.529.6732
BEER - BUDWEISER, $3.75

If you've been a David Letterman fan for awhile, then you've probably already seen the inside of the Old Town Bar. Remember when Dave was on NBC way back when Drew Barrymore was still in a diaper and Monica Lewinsky was just a gleam in Bill Clinton's cigar? Well, in the opening of his old show, a camera snaked through a bar, and this is the bar that it snaked through. When you visit the bar in person, you'll see that the Old Town Bar lives up to its name. The long wooden bar, the dusty antique-looking mirror behind it and the tables and booths all look like relics from a tavern your grandfather used to swill booze at. The clientele is mainly regulars, and you can count on the place to be packed every day after working hours (6:30 to 9:00) with a crowd ranging from suits to hardhats. After nine, it's less crowded and easier to belly up to the bar, but think twice if you're packing a cell phone. There's a sign hanging from the bar declaring, "No Cell Phones!" A cell-phone-free island in a city that's brimming over with assholes yakking on those godawful machines, that's reason enough to thank whatever God you happen to pray to when the plane hits heavy turbulence for the Old Town Bar.

6:30 P.M. I'm heading up 6th Avenue toward The Tomato Bar when I see a Mister Softee truck parked on the corner. And when I say the words *Mister Softee* I say them with the utmost respect, admiration and love—yes, love—that one man can have for another without the Moral Majority showing up at his door with rope and a burning cross at the ready. In a world where everybody's popping Viagra like M&M's, trying to prove what a stud they are, here comes a guy with the solid brass balls to call himself Mister Softee. It's so rare in this day of lying politicians and ex-pro football players who chop their wives heads off and then claim they didn't and then get off scot-free, to find a real man like Mister Softee, who's willing to label himself in such a truthful and honest manner. He could care less if he can't get it up, he's Mister Softee and if you don't

like it, well, then you can just go eat a leper's ass. For those of you who are about to admire a *real* man like Mister Softee, we salute you!

THE TOMATO BAR

676 SIXTH AVE. @ 21ST ST.

212.645.6525

BEER - BUDWEISER, $3.50

Walking into The Tomato Bar after seeing the Mister Softee truck is the holy mother of all buzz kills. You'd think a place that names itself The Tomato would have all sorts of wacky tomato knick-knacks, special tomato drinks, tomato swizzle sticks, tomato wallpaper and maybe even some sort of kooky homage to ketchup. But no. I walk in and there's your standard wooden bar. There are no tomato knickknacks on it. There's your standard bartender. He doesn't offer to tell you of any tomato drink specials. The walls are covered with green-leaf wallpaper. There's no tomato wallpaper. I was hoping that on the bar they'd have those ketchup-flavored potato sticks to munch on. There are no ketchup-flavored potato sticks in the bar here. And to add biting insult to painful injury, there are dining tables behind me and not one of them has a bottle of ketchup sitting on it. What kind of a mind fuck is going on here? Screw the flowers, I want to know where all the tomatoes have gone? Can someone answer me? Where have all the freaking tomatoes gone? Answer me, goddammit! At this horrible and depressing moment of my life, I'm thankful for one thing and one thing only: At least Mister Softee isn't here to see this tavern of deceit, this barroom of lies, this den of distortion. You say "Tomato". . .I say, "False Advertising!"

7:25 P.M. I'm taking the number 9 uptown train to Times Square. It's almost 7:30 at night and I've only drank five beers so far. Time for some speed drinking to get my 13-beer quota in as quick as I can. This day has been filled with too many bone-crushing defeats: The hellish and scathing heat index which continues to climb further every day, the loss of the cab, the wrath of the Japanese Town Car driver, the dreaded Waffle in a Bag, the puke-inducing Apricot Summer Ale, the brutish sock salesman and, of course, the tomatoless Tomato Bar. Sure, there's been a modicum of minor victories: No hangover in the morning, the cell phone ban at Old Town and, of course, the Mister Softee sighting. But the scales are woefully tipped in favor of defeat. I mean, for the love of God, can someone *please* tell me why anyone would put a waffle in a bag?

ESPN ZONE

1472 BROADWAY @ 42ND ST.

212.921.ESPN

BEER - COORS LIGHT, $4.00

"Ladies and gentlemen, on today's *Springer,* 'Cementheads and the Women Who Love Them!' "

A BAR NAMED FOR A CABLE CHANNEL. WHAT'S NEXT, A PHARMACY NAMED AFTER THE SOAP OPERA NETWORK?

8:00 P.M. I've just bought two meat-on-a-stick things from the meat-on-a-stick-thing-stand guy. If you've never lived in or visited New York, you don't know what the meat-on-stick things are. Basically, they're sticks with hunks of charbroiled meat stuck on them. It's the sort of thing vegetarians' most horrific nightmares are made out of. If I had to sum up the meat-on-stick things in 14 words or less, I'd have to say, they're a delicious meat snack and perfect for the bar critic on the go. In summation I would like to say: Bon apetit, muy bueno and hasta la vista to you each morning. Nest pa? Quandro, donde est strehlo!

PIG 'N' WHISTLE

165 W. 47TH ST. BETWEEN 6TH AND 7TH AVES.
212.302.0110
BEER - BECK'S, $4.50

This legendary Times Square bar has a curious mix of locals and tourists in it. Maybe *curious* isn't the right word. Perhaps *peculiar* would be a better choice. Or *strange*. *Queer* would work. As would *unusual*. You know what word I like? *Odd*. It's a nice compact three-letter word. It's succinct, yet descriptive. It's a dependable word housed in a small package. It's like the Volkswagen Beetle in the wondrous world of words. Remember the Bee Gees song "Words?" I had that 45 when I was a kid. But then I traded all my 45's and a huge box of old *Mad* magazines for an ounce of pot when I was a 16-year-old, know-it-all punk. How stupid! I had old Beatles 45's on the Capitol label that would be worth a lot of money today. And those old *Mad*'s from the '60s? God I hate to think what those things would be worth. But, you know, at 16 I thought I had outgrown all of that. Stupid. Stupid, stupid, stupid! Although I do have to say in my own

Pig 'n' Whistle

BE SAFE • KEEP COVER CLOSED

defense, it *was* really good weed. Oh, I almost forgot the Pig 'n' Whistle review. Uh. . .let's see, I'm almost done with my beer, so I better make this quick. . .uhh. . .John Belushi used to hang out here when he was on *Saturday Night Live.* He doesn't hang out here anymore.

8.50 P.M. I'm walking up Broadway just past 53rd Street when I get stuck behind the most dreaded of all things in midtown Manhattan, the out-of-town tourist family. The tourist family is usually a tightly knit group of one father, one mother and roughly two to four children whose ages range between 7 and 16. They're always dressed in bright and somewhat offensive colors, and at least 50 percent of the family is grossly overweight. They're armed with city and subway maps, disposable cameras, and all are carrying shopping bags stuffed with miniature plastic Statue of Liberty replicas, ridiculously large pencils with "New York" inscribed on them and Hard Rock Cafe T-shirts which translated into the eyes of a mugger is a giant neon sign flickering above them saying, "Please mug us. We have lots of cash and zero street smarts."

The family I'm stuck behind consists of a mother and father in their mid to late thirties. The father has a '70s style moustache, a mullet hairdo that's just beginning to get gray at the temples, a gut that's threatening to bust out of his gray Nike T-shirt, white shorts, dark socks and sandals that belong on a monk who's just pledged silence for the next decade. Mom is short, just over five feet, and is sporting a brown Dorothy Hamill bob. She's wearing a multicolored "New York" T-shirt and probably spent the better part of the morning squeezing herself into her tight jeans that make her ass that's bigger than a fin off of a '55 Cadillac even more pronounced. They have three children, two boys and one girl, who appear to all be preteen. They're average-looking kids except for their alarming, choppy, off-center, Tex Watson-like haircuts. Looks like dad got a Flobee for Christmas last year. Of course they're all fanned out, holding hands and hogging the whole sidewalk. And to top it all off, they're slow walkers. They're moving at a pace that would put a slug to sleep, and I'm stuck behind them. And mom's complaining in a whiny voice that it "stinks in this city, can't they do something about the smell?" I just want to grab her and scream in her face, "Where did you think you were coming to? Of course it stinks here, everybody pisses all over the place, there's garbage and vomit overflowing out of every trash can and you know that homeless guy you pretended not to see a block ago? He's probably got bowel movements in his pants that are older than your youngest son. This is New York. If you don't like smelly, shit-strewn cities, why in holy hell's fire did you decide to come here instead of the Wisconsin Dells like your neighbors? And for the love of strange footwear, pick up the pace! Did you plan your entire vacation with the intent of slowing me down?"

I wisely decide to leave them be, no need in risking a summons from Adolf. . .err. . .Mayor Giuliani for disrupting a tourist. Instead I cross over to Seventh Avenue and once again resume a pace befitting a journalist on the prowl. . .a man who's *truly* on the move.

BRIDGES BAR (IN THE HILTON HOTEL)

1335 6TH AVE. @ 54TH ST.

212.586.7000

BEER - BLUE MOON BELGIAN WHITE, $6.00

This is a large bar in the Hilton. It's got low lighting, a large circular bar and several TV sets hanging from the ceiling. It's loaded with tourists, but a decent bar all the same. Plus they've got a really tasty bowl of free snack mix on the bar. Somewhere in the distance I can faintly hear Eric Clapton confessing for the umpteenth time that he shot the sheriff. I'm sitting here wondering why he shot the sheriff, yet he "didn't shoot the deputy." I mean, you've already killed the sheriff, if you get caught, that's it. Ba-da-boom, ba-da-bing. A lifetime of go-to-jail cards are thrown at your feet. So you might as well blast the deputy's brains all over the jailhouse wall as well. I mean, go nuts wild man, you're already going to the big house, you might as well make sure you make the front page. As I'm mulling these facts over, a woman sits down next to me and orders a cup of coffee in a very sultry and slinky voice dripping with a Southern accent. God, how I love to type the words "sultry" and "slinky." Anyway, I turn slightly and there sits a woman with long blonde hair down to the small of her back—God, how I love to type in the words "small of her back"—she's very pretty, she sort of looks like Cheri Oteri who used to be on *Saturday Night Live* whom I've had many unusual and repulsive sexual fantasies about. Some involve leather, feather dusters and rope, others don't. She appears to be in her late twenties to early thirties and is dressed conservatively in a white blouse and black skirt which stops just short of her delightful kneecap. While she's dressed conservatively, her blouse has the top four buttons undone, and if I lean back just slightly I can see her white bra, which houses a perky bosom. I'm sure you know by now I love to type the words "perky bosom," so why waste time telling you. While I'm trying to get a better look into her shirt, she turns slightly, our eyes meet and she says, "Hello."

Oh. My. God. She said hello. To me. I swiftly recover from the shock and say hello back.

She asks if I just got in town and I tell her no, I live here. I ask where she's from and she tells me Memphis. I've been to Memphis a couple of times, so we talk about Graceland and Beale Street. She tells me her name is Lucy. She doesn't seem to have much of a sense of humor, but that's okay. She has perky breasts and she's probably leaving town in a couple of days, so I'll never see have to see her again after I talk her into performing humiliating sexual acts with me. This is the stuff that *Penthouse* Forum letters are made from. She's talking, but I'm not really listening; I'm wondering if she has big nipples. I'm hoping for those ones that look like silver dollars. Those are good. But seconds later nine scary words burst my nipple balloon: "Have you let the Lord Jesus into your life?"

"Umm. . .excuse me?" I ask, crash landing back to reality while taking a long pull of my beer.

"Have you let the Lord Jesus into your life?" she asks while smiling that big, goofy grin that can only belong to the born-again Christian who wants to convert the world.

Now, I have nothing against born-again Christians, but I know that born-again Christians probably aren't going to show me their silver-dollar nipples anytime in the near future. I also know that born-again Christians mean well, but born-again Christians aren't going to do the Hoppity Hooper dance in the nude with their perky breasts bouncing up and down, up and down, up and down. I had to make a move.

"Oh geez, look at the time," I say while looking at my wrist, which is embarrassingly void of a watch. "I gotta get going."

"Let me give you a pamphlet," she offers while digging in her purse, her face locked into the born-again Christian, Moonie-like grin.

"Umm," I stammer while grabbing my bag, "I really can't, you know, the war and all. . ."

I don't really know what *that* was supposed to mean, but it confused her enough to allow me to escape unscathed and unsaved. Praise Jesus!

9:30 P.M. Silver-dollar nipples. . .silver-dollar nipples. . .silver-dollar nipples. . .

OLD CASTLE PUB

160 W. 54TH ST. @ 7TH AVE.

212.471.4860

BEER - BUDWEISER

It doesn't get much more boring and mundane than this place. There's nothing to write about here. Aside from the bar and the bartender who just served me my beer, it's one of those midtown places that's boring as. . .well, midtown. Everything's light brown in here. At this moment your amateur bar critic would be perplexed, puzzled and pissing in his pants. Because what can you write about when there's absolutely nothing to say? The amateur

74

critic would probably try to cover up by throwing out colorful and jaunty adjectives like, "friable," "normative," "commensurable" and, of course, "soup." Even though soup is not an adjective: as we all know it's a savory, mainly liquid food. Being a professional who's totally in control, I don't need to stoop to such pedestrian, Ted Mack amateur-hour tricks. Nope, I know from years of experience that when faced with a situation like this it's better to simply type in the word "huzzah!" and then move onward. So. . .huzzah!

10:15 P.M. As I wander up 54th Street, I spy a man packing up a table of books he was selling. I stop and see a paperback copy of *The New American Desk Encyclopedia* on top of a box.

"How much for the encyclopedia?" I ask the bookseller who vaguely resembles my sixth-grade science teacher, Mr. Manning, who himself resembled the pipe-smoking TV dad of *Dennis the Menace.*

"Two dollars," he said, not even looking up from his packing to quote the price. I was impressed by that, so I paid the two bucks without haggling. I took the book and underneath a streetlight I looked up the words "silver-dollar nipples." Sadly there was no such entry. The closest thing was "Silverfish." According to the encyclopedia, Silverfish are "any of various wingless insects of the order *Thysanura.* One common variety, *Lepisma saccharina,* has two long antennae, three barbed tail parts, and silver-to-gray scales."

I knew that.

THE OAK ROOM

768 5TH AVE. @ 59TH ST.

212.546.5330

BEER - BUDWEISER, $4.00

Do you like oak, Jimmy?

11:00 P.M. I'm taking a cab over to the East Side in hopes of finding a bar that has something interesting going for it. I'm reading about saxifrage in my copy of *The New American Desk Encyclopedia*. It says that saxifrage is a group of small rock plants whose leaves grow in a rosette at the base of the stem and whose flowers grow in clusters at the tip of the stem. It goes on to explain that the name "saxifrage" means stone breaker and they once were believed to cure kidney stones.

I knew that.

RATHBONES

1702 2ND AVE. @ 88TH ST.

212.369.7361

BEER - MILLER LITE, $3.50

TUESDAY

Rathbones is part Irish bar and part sports bar. There's sawdust on the floor. The place reminds me a little of the bar on *Bonanza* where Hoss used to drink. Which kind of makes sense, because remember the episode with Hoss and the little leprechauns? God, I love it when things come together like this. Don't you?

A Friendly Tavern with Excellent Food.

BE SAFE ✧ KEEP COVER CLOSED

11:45 P.M. I know I've been writing this every day, but the heat just refuses to break. It's almost midnight, I'm still sweating bullets and the beer is starting to hit me. Luckily, there are two bars within spitting distance. Unluckily, one of them is yet *another* Irish bar and the other is Elaine's, the hangout for the Upper East Side's once-elite power brokers who are now older than Bob Hope's six iron.

AND ALL THIS TIME I THOUGHT I WAS SEEING DOUBLE.

MARTY O'BRIEN'S

1696 2ND AVE. BETWEEN 87TH & 88TH STS.

BEER - BUDWEISER, $4.00

This is a very small place, it's dark and there are two drunken guys hovering over their beers at the bar. One of them is trying to sing along with the Van Morrison song "And It Stoned Me." The bartender is staring out the window, probably wondering what he did in a former lifetime to deserve this. The other guy is just about ready to fall off his bar stool. And me, well, I'd love to stay, but not really, so I'm leaving. Too-ra-loo-ra-fucking-loo-ra. Or something just like that.

12:05 A.M. One more beer and one more bar, then it's home to pass out while visions of Alka Seltzer and silver-dollar nipples dance through my dreams.

IT'S A BAR. . .IT'S AN OLD FOLKS HOME. . .IT'S TWO, TWO, TWO PLACES
I DON'T WANT TO BE AT IN ONE!

ELAINE'S

1703 2ND AVE. BETWEEN 88TH & 89TH STS.

212.534.8103

BEER - BUDWEISER, $4.00

And on the eighth day God created Grecian Formula.

1:19 A.M. I'd like to end this chapter with a fun verb. Something like, "repatriated."

WEDNESDAY

HAIKU-KA-CHOO

3:45 P.M. I've been awake since around 12:30 p.m. The reason I haven't made an entry yet is I've got very troubling, upsetting and quite painful news and I'm finding it hard to write the words. I guess the best way out of this is just to come right out and say it, so here goes: I've got a rash on my ass.

Whew. . .I did it. And you know what? I feel better. I was thinking about not writing about it because it's a little embarrassing—actually, it puts the ass back in embarrass—but I've promised total honesty in this book, and by the love of sweet gum, that's what I'm going to deliver. So now you know. Obviously, it's from the heat; I've been sweating a lot and now my ass is covered with a red, prickly rash. If you spend three days waltzing around drinking beer in sweat-soaked underwear, a rash is almost certain to appear. I knew that going into this assignment—I was going to write that this puts the ass back into assignment, but then decided not to beat a dying, if not already dead horse—so I'll just have to deal with it. You do the crime, be ready to do the time. Anyway, I'm experienced when it comes to ass mishaps. A couple of years ago I had a hemorrhoid that felt like the S.S. Minnow had landed in my butt. As much as you probably don't want to hear the particulars of this upcoming hemorrhoid story, well, believe me, it hurt me worse than it's going to hurt you, so here goes.

It all started when I was out drinking with my friend Eugenia—you remember her, she's the one from the story about running out of a bar from the Sunday chapter. Anyway, we were sitting in the Motor City Bar in the East Village, drinking beer and talking with some of the regulars around the bar. There was an ad on the TV for the Jerry Lewis telethon and I wondered aloud how much money had been raised in the duration of all the telethons. We decided it had to be close to a billion dollars, so I jokingly said that maybe they should move on to a new disease. They didn't seem to be having too much luck with that one. Well, everybody got all upset, said I was making fun of the handicapped, and they all were telling me to shut up, so naturally I kept talking about it. It's not like I was the first one to ever make that observation. I've heard stand-up comics make similar jokes, but the crowd at Motor City was not having any of it. Eugenia was laughing, but said that karma would pay me back if I didn't stop it. So of course I kept up my little telethon monologue—not that I enjoy making fun of diseased people, but because it was freaking everyone out so much. But two days later when it felt like I had a horn growing out of my ass, I realized Eugenia was right. I've never had a hemorrhoid so big and painful in my life. It felt only slightly smaller than the pint-sized thespian Gary Coleman. After a couple of pain-riddled days I kicked my pride to the curb and went to the doctor.

There's nothing more embarrassing than having a doctor check out a hemorrhoid, and this was no exception to this most horrific of all rules. On this occasion, my doctor had me take off my pants and underwear and instructed me to lay on my side on one of those leather bed things in doctors' offices that are always covered with paper. Then he slipped latex rubber gloves on and probed around in there for awhile. Now that was uncomfortable enough, but that was just the coming attraction before the nightmarish main event that was to follow.

The doctor told me to lay flat on my stomach, and being the dutiful patient, I complied with his wishes. Then he left the room, and minutes later he came back with a plastic rod that was at least 10 inches long. He walked over to my face, held the rod out, wagged it under my nose and then hit a switch and the rod lit up. It looked like something Darth Vader would prance around with in his living room. And then the good doctor calmly, slowly and somewhat maniacally said the words that many men—myself included—hope never to have to hear in their lives: "I'm going to put this inside of your anus now."

"I. . .I. . .I," was all I was able to stammer out. I wanted to say, "I really don't want you to do that," but before I could spit it out, he was already violating me with the Darth Vader rod. It felt like he had that thing inside of me for five minutes beyond eternity. Finally, after he robbed me of my final shred of dignity, he took it out and in a cold, calculated voice told me to get dressed. He ended up giving me some cream in a silver foil tube and told me to sit in a hot bathtub every night until the swelling went down. I've had nightmares about the Darth Vader rod ever since. And I switched doctors.

And now I've got a rash on my ass, and I didn't even make fun of Jerry's telethon this time. It's just not fair, but sometimes these are the cards that life deals you. A weaker, less experienced writer would quit at this point, but not me. I'm halfway through this 99 beers adventure, and there's no turning back.

The temperature is 95 degrees outside, so I've decided to put a spare pair of underwear in my bag in an effort to keep my ass dry and sideline this nasty, horrible and most embarrassing rash. It's going to feel a little odd traveling the streets of Manhattan with underwear packed in my bag next to my cigarettes, but it's a necessary evil. I don't know if they stick a rod up your ass over a rash, but I'll be goddamned if I'm going to find out.

(Author's Note: In my somewhat obsessive quest to finally have a successful theme day, I decided to write all the reviews for Wednesday in haiku. Of course these will be written in the genuine, tried and true five-syllable, seven-syllable, five-syllable old-world-style haiku. None of this reckless and dangerous "any number of syllables will do" haiku nonsense that the kids are all so fond of these days.)

SPAIN

113 W. 13TH ST. @ 6TH AVE.

212.929.9580

BEER - BUDWEISER, $3.50

Two old people drink

Bartender very old too

Peanuts on the bar

4:35 P.M. I'm making a pit stop at the Rite Aid drug store on the corner of 13th and 6th to buy some powder to put on my rash-infested ass. I've been out less than an hour in this unbear-

NOT THE MOST EXCITING BAR IN THE CITY, BUT GOSH-DARN-IT-ALL, WHAT A HANDSOME AWNING, HUH?

able heat and already my underwear, along with the rest of my clothing, is soaked in sweat. I need to find a top-shelf ass powder containing a highly charged drying agent.

As I walk into the Rite Aid, my eardrums are immediately assaulted by Phil Collins singing "Against All Odds." Isn't it strange how 8 times out of 10 when you walk into a Rite Aid, Phil Collins will be on the store's sound system, yet you're never *really* properly prepared for it. There's no need to dwell on this fact, better to just keep your head low and move on in a swift, sweeping fashion. Bull-in-the-ring time, Johnny, bull-in-the-ring time.

Okay, I'm cruising up and down the aisles trying to find the powder section, but so far no luck. There's lots of weird items in here, but so far the strangest one I've encountered has been the "Dr. Grabow Royal Duke Filter Pipe." I'm trying to figure out just what sort of man toils through all those years of medical school and then ends up a maker of pipes? I would think a year or two of woodshop in high school and you'd be qualified to be a freaking *master* pipe maker. Golly, Dr. Grabow, *nice* life decision. And I hope you take that with all the sarcasm that was intended. Now turn your head and cough.

Finally I find the powder section. It's in between the Q-Tips and The Rite Aid Baby Wipes. There are many choices, mostly products manufactured by the Johnson & Johnson company. I don't know about you, but there's no fucking way I'm trusting my ass to a company with such a redundant name like Johnson & Johnson. Couldn't they have come up with something a little more inventive, like Johnson Squared, or Johnson to the Second Power?

Oh, look at this, Caldesene Protecting Powder For Babies & Adults. The word *Protecting* literally jumps out at me like a jackrabbit in heat. The pink plastic bottle is the perfect size (five ounces) for traveling, it's a bargain at just $5.19 and just below the logo it promises, "Two Way Action." You've got to love that. I'm not exactly sure why, but you've just got to. Love it, that is.

CALIENTE CAB CO.

61 7TH AVE. S. @ BLEECKER ST.

212.243.8517

BEER - DOS EQUIS, $5.00

Mexican frat house

Drunk people drinking loudly

I don't like it here

5:30 P.M. I never thought I would write these words, and I pray to whatever gods are floating around out there that I never have to again, but I'm preparing to powder my ass in the Caliente Cab Co. bathroom. There's only one stall in here and it's really cramped. It's not really a stall at all. They've fastened a steel half door to a corner in the room directly opposite the urinal. It's kind of triangular in shape, and there's not much more room than in a telephone booth. It feels like a bathroom on an airplane, and God how I hate to fly. This is not good, but my ass needs to be powdered and it needs to be powdered right now. So on with the show we go.

I know you probably don't want a mental picture of what's going on, but here it is. My pants are around my knees and I'm trying to pat the powder on, but it doesn't feel like it's adhering to. . .well. . .you know, the ass. All of a sudden it hits me like a fish monger slapping me on the cheek with a raw tuna—what I need to do is to line my underwear with the protective powder. And that's what I've done. Visions of Al Pacino in *Scarface* fly through my head as I pull my pants up and see all the white powder on the floor. Some drunk will probably stumble in here later and snort this stuff off the floor.

As I walk out of the Caliente I can feel the powder already performing its magic. It's soothing and refreshing all at once. I feel somewhat like Björk walking down the Oscar red carpet in one of her duck dresses. Oh, I feel so. . .so. . .protected!

5:45 P.M. Thoughts while heading uptown to Times Square on a full, but not jampacked number 1 train: My ass isn't burning, but it's starting to itch again. . .I wonder what the woman next to me would do if she knew I had a pair of spare underwear in my bag. . .wouldn't it be weird if she had a pair of her underwear in *her* bag. . ."and you coming back to me is against all odds". . .goddamned Phil Collins songs, you can *never* get them out of your head. . .look at those tits!. . .I think I'll have something with cheese on it for dinner.

WWF
(WORLD WRESTLING FEDERATION)
NEW YORK

1501 BROADWAY @ 43RD ST.
212.398.2563
BEER - BUDWEISER, $4.00

Wrestling and booze bar
Men with low I.Q.'s abound
I want to leave now

OBVIOUSLY THIS BRUTE IS TURNING A DEAF EAR TO THE AGE-OLD, "NO SHIRT, NO SHOES, NO SERVICE" RULE.

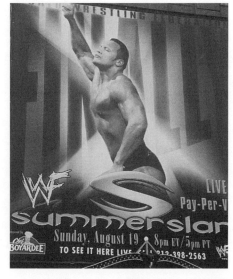

6:25 P.M. I'm standing in front of Tad's Steaks on Broadway between 44th and 45th Streets and I'm examining the sign in the window. It reads, "Wow! 8 oz. T-Bone only $6.99 + tax! Includes baked potato, garlic bread and fresh salad." Well. . .wow, indeed.

Every time I pass a Tad's Steaks questions invariably spin around in my head like a frisbee gone somewhat amok. Who is Tad? Does he have a last name? Does he have friends? Does A-1 sauce flow through his veins like a coursing river during the nasty and treacherous monsoon season? Does he realize that his name spelled backwards is Dat? As in—and feel free to sing along kids—"Gimmee dat ding, gimmee dat ding, gimmee gimme dat, gimmee gimmee dat, gimmee dat ding." And finally, how does Tad mend a broken heart? How does he stop the sun from shining? What make's Tad's world go round?" Questions, questions everywhere, but alas, there are no answers, only the nagging need to keep moving. Keep on moving.

LANGAN'S

150 W. 47TH ST. @ 7TH AVE.

212.869.5482

BEER - BUDWEISER, $4.50

New York Post hangout

Steve Dunleavy is not here

Nightcrawler either

7:15 P.M. I thought for sure *New York Post* columnist Steve Dunleavy would be at Langan's. According to his column he practically lives at this midtown bar and restaurant. My plan was to approach him and ask if I could interview him. I figured he'd either let me or he might be all boozed up and punch me in the nose. Either way it would've made for great copy here. Quite unlike the mundane words that are falling onto paper now. Maybe you don't know who Steve Dunleavy is. Well, that doesn't

WEDNESDAY

matter anymore, because I couldn't find the son of a bitch anyway. He's always supposed to be here; they've put up a freaking monument to the guy in this bar. But on the day I need him, he's nowhere to be found. Great. Thanks, Steve, I think I'll just buy a *Daily News* tomorrow and skip the *Post*.

And now my ass is starting to burn a little. That motherfucking ass powder *promised* protection. Godammit! I stand here on the corner of 50th Street and Broadway in this godawful 93 degree temperature with sweat dripping from every stinking inch of my body wishing, just like John Lennon did before that nut case blew his brains all over the Dakota's driveway, that someone would give me some truth. Actually, John Lennon said, "*Gimmee* some truth." But that's a little pedestrian, don't you think?

TWIST (IN THE AMERITANIA HOTEL)

230 W. 54TH ST. @ BROADWAY

212.247.500

BEER - ROLLING ROCK, $3.50

Small hip hotel bar

Home of the best martini

I'm drinking a beer

8:05 P.M. I stopped at a deli to get some cigarettes, and I also grabbed a "snack size" bag of cookies to eat on my 10-block journey to Smith's bar. The cookies are Keebler's Fudge Shoppe Mini Fudge Stripe Cookies. On the back of the bag, below the ingredients, is a warning that reads: "May contain traces of peanut."

We live in a world where high school kids are blowing up their schools and shooting each other, pop stars have sex with little boys then pay their families off and go on to sell out Madison Square Garden, Washington interns go on an old-fashioned date with a scary-looking, old-enough-to-be-their-scary-father, married congressman and are never seen again, sharks are chewing up our children, publicists in SUV's are backing over the rest of us and most frightening of all, according to an investigative *Rolling Stone* piece, Britney Spears doesn't want to be treated like a little girl anymore. Yet the good people at Keebler think we're afraid of a "trace of peanut" in a cookie? Attention Keebler cookie makers: You may want to see a therapist and discuss something we like to call "paranoia." Oh, and one more thing, Keebler, concerning those cute little elves that supposedly make all your cookies and snack crackers, one word: "Bullshit."

SMITH'S

701 8TH AVE. @ 44TH ST.

212.246.3268

BEER - BUDWEISER

Truly a dive bar

Crusty, gruff old bartender

Old hooker nearby

8:50 P.M. It's time to change into my spare underwear; I can't wait a second longer. My ass itches and on the rare occasion I have the privacy to scratch it, then it starts burning. It's time to break out the spare pair I so wisely packed at the start of this day's journey. Unwisely I chose Smith's bar to change in. This

THINK OF IT AS A THEME BAR WITHOUT A THEME.

place is an old-school Hell's Kitchen dive bar and the bathroom is just as dicey as you'd expect in a place that's home to slobbering old alcoholic men and the 60-year-old, dried-up hookers who love them. There's only one stall in here and there's no door on it. Flies are buzzing everywhere, it smells and there's no seat on the toilet. I think about putting the underwear-change off, but I can't stand it for one second longer. I need my ass to be dry, even if for only a few minutes. If my ass doesn't touch dry underwear in the next three minutes, I'm going to start freaking out. And I can't be freaking out, I've still got seven bars to go to before I can allow myself the luxury of a full-blown freakout in the safety of my own apartment after I've tucked my pen and pad safely away for the night.

Luckily the bathroom was empty, so I quickly slipped off my shoes, took off my pants and replaced the sweat-soaked underwear with the dry pair in my bag without any of the old alcoholics stumbling in and creating problems that only an old drunken man with a shot liver and kidneys that have been swimming in alcohol for the better part of the last three decades can create. I'm somewhat proud that the whole operation took under two minutes, and that includes fly swatting. I feel sort of like one of those racing car crew guys who changes all four tires, checks the oil, fills up the gas tank and tunes the engine up in 14 seconds at the Indianapolis 500.

My ass is now covered in dry underwear. Hot fucking damn. Sweet, sweet joy! Immediately the rash feels much better. The only problem now is what to do with the sweat-soaked, powder caked pair that I'm holding in my hand. And yes, you read right, they're *caked* with that rotten powder that promised to protect. Not only did the powder not protect, it formed a shell on my underwear that probably did more harm than good. I'm leaving the pink bottle on top of the toilet. Let the drunken patrons of Smith's enjoy the powder's "Two Way Action." I still don't know what that means, but I can't worry about that now—I've got to figure out what to do with this underwear.

There's no way I'm putting them back into my bag. It was weird enough walking around with a pair of fresh underwear in my bag; I'm certainly not traveling around this city with a sweaty, smelly, powder-caked pair. The only choices are to throw them in the garbage can or to flush them down the toilet. There are problems with each of these decisions, and they are as follows: If I chuck them in the garbage can, there's a good chance that one of these decrepit, old, alcoholic regulars may find them, as they probably root through the garbage on a more than regular basis. How do I know this? Trust me, everyone in this god-forsaken tavern has that certain look that can only grace the face of a seasoned garbage-can rooter. It's a certain *je ne sais quoi*, that one can spot if you hang out in dive bars long enough. God only knows what these booze-addled derelicts would do with a pair of sweaty underwear. It boggles the mind. I'd go into detail, but I'm sure with my unending ass-writing in this chapter I've already more than surpassed my allotted reader-gross-out factor, so let's just say it wouldn't be pleasant if my underwear made its way into the hands of one of these stumbling, bumbling, booze-swilling social misfits. The thoughts would haunt me for months if not years.

The other choice is to flush them down the toilet. The problem with this is that this action could clog the toilet up, causing it to overflow and make a mess in the bathroom. As I swat at a swarm of flies, look at the garbage on the floor and breathe in the stench that's rising from the uncleaned toilet, I throw the pair in the bowl, flush it and run out of the bar before the bathroom starts flooding. As I make it outside, I salute Smith's bar and bid them a gentle, yet meaningful, "Ta ta."

COLLINS

735 8TH AVE. BETWEEN 46TH AND 47TH STS.

212.541.4206

BEER - BUDWEISER, $4.00

Another dive bar

Midget is drinking rum shots

I flirt with floozy

9:30 P.M. I've got to get something to eat. Those Keebler cookies aren't enough to make it through this boozefest of an

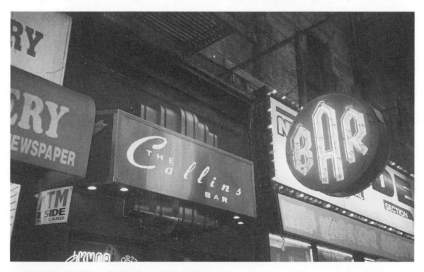

A BAR BAR BAR, BAR-BARBARA ANN.

evening. Even though I did detect a slight trace of peanut in them. I'm trying to figure out where to go. My budget is tight because due to an uneven schedule I've got to be traveling via cab a few times, and that will chew up expenses. I'm pondering my situation when the word *Wow* comes stumbling into my brain. And I think we all know what follows. . ."8 oz. T-Bone only $6.99 + tax! Includes baked potato, garlic bread and fresh salad!" Wow.

9:40 P.M. The line is about 10 people deep as I stroll into the Times Square Tad's Steakhouse. Tad's is set up like a high school cafeteria. You wait in line, grab a plastic red tray and place your order with someone standing behind the counter. You have to stand there and wait for your meal, then you make your way toward the cash register, passing plastic containers housing a variety of different kinds of cake and pie and bottles of soda, juice and beer sitting in a vat of ice.

So far I haven't made it very close to the counter where you order. In fact, I've been pushed back a space by some guy who's about 6 foot 7, looks like he's spent every waking moment of his pathetic life lifting weights and has a square head complete with a flat-top hairdo to accentuate the squareness of his iron-skillet-like thick skull. He's wearing a Gold's Gym muscle shirt, grey sweatpants and big black shitkicker boots. I took my place at the end of the line and moments later the big galoot is clomping my way and then he walks in front of me.

"Excuse me, the end of the line starts behind me," I say to Squarehead in a calming manner so as not to get killed.

"Uhh, oh, well I uhh, had to put some money in a meter. I uhh, was here a couple of minutes ago before uhh, you got here," he explained in gruff, Neanderthal tones.

"Whatever," I said, realizing, that even if I won this battle I wouldn't be able to properly enjoy the $6.99 8 oz. T-bone with a busted jaw.

It takes about five minutes to get close to the spot at the counter where you order. The meals are numbered and are listed on signs that hang over the counter area. I was preparing myself to order the number 8, which is the 8 oz. T-Bone, baked potato, garlic bread and fresh salad all for only $6.99. Wow.

As we approach the counter man taking the orders, Squarehead orders the number 2. I scan the signs and see that the number two is called "The Big One." Which is the giant size T-Bone with an asking price of $12.95.

I immediately started thinking to myself, "I bet you ask for the "big one" from all the guys, huh Squarehead." And "It figures a big shitkicker like yourself orders the number 2." And, "Is that a "Big One" on your platter or are you just glad to see me, Squarehead." I'm really cracking myself up here, and all of a sudden as I'm trying to suppress my laughter I end up making one of those snort nose sounds that comes out when you're trying to hold back a laugh. Squarehead shoots a look my way, and I start coughing and say, "Smoky in here, huh?"

It takes Squarehead about three minutes to process that last statement, and by the time he does, my steak arrives in all its 8 oz. glory. And Squarehead is royally pissed.

"Hey, uhh, I ordered before him, where's uhh, my order?" he barks out to the Hispanic counter man who appears to have trouble processing any English other than the dinner numbers of 1 through 10.

While the counter man was trying to figure out Squarehead's words of protest, I broke in and said, "I think it's because you ordered the 'Big One.' It's a bigger cut and probably takes longer to cook." The Hispanic counter man was shaking his head wildly in agreement, even though I don't think he understood a word of what I was saying.

"Uhh," was all Squarehead could muster as I walked around him and toward the cash register. "Enjoy your steak, when you finally get it," I said as I walked around him.

"Uhh," he grunted at me while looking wounded. His shoulders sunk and his head dropped just like a man thrown off a pedestal.

Even a squarehead knows that you can't knock a man's block off for telling him to enjoy his meal, but he knew what I meant and there wasn't jack shit he could do about it. I won. Ha! I take a table in the corner and smother my paper-thin T-Bone in A-1 sauce. Good God how I love the smell of A-1 sauce in the evening, it smells like. . .victory.

Wow.

KENNEDY'S

327 W. 57TH ST. BET 8TH AND 9TH STS.

212.759.4242

BEER - GUINNESS, $4.00

Love this Irish bar

Though I'm sick of Irish bars

I know the owner

10:30 P.M. I'm taking a cab across town to the East Side and the driver is this crusty old man who looks like he just crawled out of a sewer. His shirt is gray, but it was probably white once, years ago. And it might've been washed once, years ago. With his

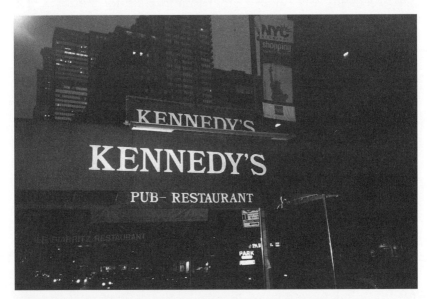

IS THIS BAR NAMED AFTER THE ASSASSINATED PRESIDENT OR THE FORMER MTV VEEJAY? YOU MAKE THE CALL!

white shocks of hair sticking out willy-nilly, he looks a little like an unbathed Professor Irwin Corey, if you remember him. If not, well, just picture a crazy old man and then picture him a little crazier and you're getting close. The only consolation is he smells worse than me. And when you really think about it, what kind of consolation is that?

He's talking to himself, but I can't hear what he's saying because he's got a classic rock radio station blaring in the cab. It's louder than Blue Cheer with their Marshall stacks turned up to 12 in here. I'd ask him if he's deaf, but I'm not going to because I think he's deaf and he wouldn't be able to hear me anyway. The song that's playing is "Shock the Monkey" by Peter Gabriel. I've never really listened to it closely before, and now being forced to hear it at this eardrum-piercing level, I find it a most disturbing song. Why in blazing hellsfire would anyone want to shock a monkey? I like monkeys. They're cute and fun. They mean no one any harm. You know what's more fun than a barrelful of monkeys? Nothing. Nada. Bupkiss. The defining moment of fun *is* a barrelful of monkeys. And rock singer Peter Gabriel is suggesting that we run out and start shocking these creatures who's main purpose in life is to bring fun to the world? Sorry, Peter, that's not going to be an addition to my Dayrunner anytime in the near future.

Maybe Peter's a little pissed that the Rite Aid drug stores are playing his old Genesis bandmate Phil Collins' songs on their loudspeakers but not his, so he wants to rid the world of fun by running around and shocking monkeys. Well here's a little hint on getting Rite Aid airplay, Peter: Stop singing about shocking monkeys! For God's sake, get a grip and find a different song subject. Maybe cover "Sussudio" or something. Just leave those cute little monkeys alone. Please.

Jimmy Walker's Ale House

245 E. 55TH ST. BETWEEN 2ND AND 3RD AVES.

212.319.6650

BEER - BUDWEISER, $3.50

How tempting it is

To write the word *Dy-no-mite!*

Oops, I just wrote it

11:20 P.M. I'd like to shock Peter Gabriel is what I'd like to do. Give that rotten, evil bastard a full spoonful of his own bitter, foul medicine. And no, Peter, you'll get no spoonful of sugar accompanying it either. . .you ass. God have mercy on those poor little monkeys that he's probably shocking right at this moment. Those poor, poor little monkeys.

Headlines

1678 1ST AVE. BETWEEN 87TH AND 88TH STS.

212.426.6309

BEER - BUDWEISER, $4.00

And now this just in

Yuppie guys acting like jerks

And smoking cigars

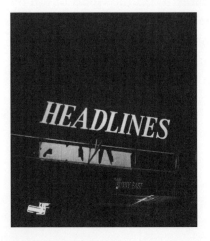

12:05 P.M. I'm starting to fade. My booze is soaked in brains. Luckily it's just a hop, skip and a sweat to. . .

WHO'S ON FIRST

1683 1ST AVE. @ 87TH ST.

212.410.2780

BEER - BUDWEISER, $3.50

I know who's on first

This frat-boy bar is on first

I smell chicken wings

12:25 A.M. One singular thought runs through my disheveled brain as my cab zooms about 90 miles per hour toward downtown Manhattan and I'm trying to ignore the fact that the wild-eyed driver has probably had more than a few puffs of crack, and that thought is this: Those poor, *poor* little monkeys.

STONED CROW

85 WASHINGTON PL.

BETWEEN 6TH AVE. AND

WASHINGTON SQ. PARK

212.677.4022

BEER - BUDWEISER, $3.50

There's no stoned crows here

What a fucking gyp this is

There's no stoned crows here

1:25 A.M. In lieu of a fun travelogue moment (translation: It's tough to have a "fun" moment when it's after one in the morning, it's still in the upper 80s, the humidity is muggy going on buggy, my head is spinning from the 12 beers I've drank, my ass is on fire and monkeys are being shocked right and left by the mean and horrible Peter Gabriel simply for the mere sport of it), I've decided to recap some of the highlights from the last three days and see what I've learned.

The recap is as follows: I've been frozen out by Irish people, I tripped a cripple, got prodded with a stick by a cab driver, I've witnessed the death of the spinning Marriott bar, I've endured the Hard Rock and Harley Davidson Cafes, I've been sexually teased by a born-again Christian with silver-dollar nipples, buckets of sweat have poured out of me, I've obsessed unnaturally over Cap'n Crunch, Colonel Sanders, sock vendors, waffles in bags and monkeys shocked by Peter Gabriel, I've drank 58 beers, suffered through brain twisting hangovers, and I've got a rash on my ass.

And what have I learned? Apparently nothing, because tomorrow I'm going to be drinking 14 more beers in 14 more bars.

PARK AVALON

225 PARK AVE. S. BETWEEN 18TH AND 19TH STS.
212.533.2500
BEER - BUDWEISER, $4.75

Snooty-ass people

Yuppies here, yuppies are there

Oh, this really sucks

2:15 A.M.   I drank thirteen beers

Now it is time to pass out

Oh, my aching ass

THE BATTLE OF
THE BARS

12:05 P.M. Advil. . .need Advil. Advil. . .

12:30 P.M. I'm scanning yesterday's notes as six Advil swim through the broken-down windmills of my aching mind, and I realize that just like Waylon and Willie, it's time to get back to the basics as far as this guide/travelogue is concerned. No more whining about the rash on my ass; even though I'm drinking 99 beers in seven days, never let it be said that *this* writer doesn't know when to say enough is enough.

A seasoned journalist like myself knows you can only do serious, in-depth, rash-on-ass writing when it's balanced out by sparkling haiku prose of the highest stripe such as was featured in yesterday's chapter—if I do unblushingly say so myself. So as the haiku reviews come to an end my huckleberry friend, so do the ass-rash entries. I'll suffer in private; God knows you've shared enough of my pain for one book. It's time to turn that frown upside down, as my second-grade teacher Sister Carol Anne used to tell me right before she'd whack me across the left cheek with a wooden ruler, and walk outside where the temperature is supposed to climb to over 100 skin-stinging degrees, think up some crackling adjectives and a peppy dangling participle or two and review some bars—my ass rash be damned!

I don't want to compare myself to Mother Teresa, but *you* probably do, so by all means, feel free.

(Author's Note: Today's chapter is a battle of similarly named bars. Hence the chapter's title, "The Battle of the Bars." So, just like Hef used to say on Playboy After Dark, *come out swinging. . .and may the best bars win.)*

1:45 P.M. Goddamnit. Sweet Lord almighty, I'm trying to keep a shiny, happy, R.E.M. face, but I tell you, sometimes when the shit hits the fan, it rains human waste like so many summer monsoons.

Once again, it's a steaming sweatbath outside. It's over 100 degrees, so I take a cab to the East Village to hit the first bar, Iggy's, on Ludlow Street. Iggy's was going to battle Iggy's Kick Ass Bar on the Upper East Side. This was going to be a battle of epic proportions. Iggy against Iggy. The Lower East Side against the Upper East Side. Good against evil. Rage against the machine. Against all odds. . .goddamn that fucking Phil Collins! Well anyway, it was to be a grand, extraordinary battle royal. I was even entertaining the thought of renting a smoke machine and arming the Iggy's bartenders with those teeny-tiny little plastic cocktail swords. I wasn't planning on going so far as to place a parrot on my shoulder, but let's just say that if one happened to land and decide to perch itself there, I wouldn't have swatted it away. But now as I walk up to the address, my heart sinks, my stomach swims and my bowels tighten. As I approach I see there's a secure steel door locking the building up. It's closed. Motherfucker of all motherfuckers.

Maybes hang heavy in the hot and sticky August air as I ponder this horrible and wretched turn of events in my battle plans. Maybe Iggy's is closed for good. Maybe it'll open in five minutes. Maybe I should come back later this evening. Maybe Iggy's is afraid of going into battle with Iggy's Kick Ass Bar. Maybe it's worthless and weak. Maybe baby I'll be true. Maybe baby I'll have you someday. Maybe I should just do what General Patton would've done had he been facing this grave and utterly bleak turn of events. Maybe I'll go to Duke's.

DUKE'S

99 E. 19TH ST. @ LEXINGTON AVE.

212.260.2922

BEER - BUDWEISER, $3.50

After mentally throwing the *I Ching* coins in my brain, I decided to replace Iggy's with Duke's bar over near 19th Street. A number of reasons factored into this quick-thinking, journalistic battle-line decision: The bar has a man's name, just like Iggy's it's

CON EDISON JUST LOVES THIS JOINT.

got five letters in the name and the fact that I'm writing phrases like "throwing the *I Ching* coins in my brain" means that I'm very much in need of a drink.

Duke's is a New Orleans southern-styled bar with a touch of frat-boy hoo-hah attitude thrown into the mix. The bar is in the front of the building with full restaurant table seating in the back. The bar area has three booths, a couple of tables and, of course, a bar. The twentysomething female bartender is a stunning blonde wearing a yellow half-shirt, white shorts, and she is equipped with a pair of giant, heaving breasts. There are a couple of good-time Charlies sitting at the end of the bar, downing longneck Budweisers while glaring drool-eyed at the bartender's massive, heaving breasts. The decor consists of vintage bar signs, old 45 vinyl records nailed willy-nilly to the ceiling, ancient beer bottle caps pasted everywhere, Christmas lights swinging from the ceiling and discarded license plates on the wall. Did I mention the blonde bartender has these huge, heaving breasts and they're pointed in my direction? And they're heaving. Did you hear me? They are heaving! *Heaving* goddamnit! Whew. The southern-styled food served here includes various burgers, ribs, fried chicken, macaroni and cheese and meatloaf just like mom used to make. My God, would you look at those bulbous, heaving breasts? Holy freaking guacamole.

VERSUS

IGGY'S KICK ASS BAR

1452 2ND AVE. @ 76TH ST.
212.327.3043
BEER - BUDWEISER, $3.50

I came here determined to hate this place because of the decidedly cornball name, but just like Mikey taking his first bite of Life cereal after his chicken-hearted older brothers were afraid to taste it, I like it! I like it!

This place is a genuine dive bar teeming with low-life atmosphere. There's a gaping, fist-sized hole in the wall over the cash register and the walls are adorned with crude, childlike drawings rendered by the drunken, booze-ravaged customers.  My personal favorite is a simplistic piece, drawn in red crayon, that reads, "Help!"

The customers range from a middle-aged, N.R.A.-styled, Chuck Heston-wannabe looking guy in a beat-up military flak jacket trying in vain to light his cigarette, to two grizzled broads in their mid-thirties who appear to have been around the block more times than a 90-year-old milkman. They're howling with laughter while guzzling booze two bar stools to my right. What they're laughing about is anybody's guess, but I'll bet maybe the joyous guffaws are partially a celebration that their diseased livers have made it through another day of an endless rain of alcohol.

It's a refreshing change of pace for this reporter to be the most sober person in the joint for once. But just seconds after I write that line, one of the grizzled broads smiles at me revealing a mouth full of brown, nicotine-stained choppers, and I realize that maybe being sober isn't necessarily a *good* thing at this point in time, but it's a refreshing change of pace all the same.

AND THE WINNER IS. . .DUKE'S!

Sure, Iggy's may kick ass. . .but did I mention the Duke's bar-tender's massive, heaving breasts? They were *heaving,* goddamnit!

4:00 P.M. T-shirt sighting on the corner of 7th Avenue and 28th Street: "Everybody Wants to Go to Heaven, But Nobody Wants to Die." While wondering what other sort of witty, golly-gee-whizbang slogans this probably-teetering-on-bankruptcy T-shirt company has come up with, I find to my delightful surprise that I'm writing some possible entries down. And look, here they are: "Everybody wants money, but nobody wants to rob a bank and then bludgeon the tellers to death with a secondhand sledgehammer once owned by prop-comic Gallagher." "Everybody wants a cheeseburger, but nobody wants to raise and then viciously slaughter a cow using only a fork, knife and a Veg-O-Matic." "Everybody wants to shop at Rite Aid, but nobody wants to listen to Phil Collins." "Everybody wants to be Colonel Sanders, but nobody wants to be Cap'n Crunch." And my personal favorite (drumroll please and thank you), "Everybody wants to drink quarts upon quarts of Nyquil, but nobody wants to suffer the tortuous sniffles and sneezes of a nasty and miserable cold."

Ah, T-shirts can be so fun. Most times they're not, but I've *heard* they can be.

MUSTANG SALLY'S

324 7TH AVE. BETWEEN 28TH AND 29TH STS.

212.695.3806

BEER - AMSTEL LIGHT, $4.00

This is one of those slightly upscale bars in midtown with a 50-50 mix of boring-ass business guys with red faces and navy blue pinstripe suits complaining about their boring-ass "executive decisions of the day" to their younger, female, tipsy-on-five-Cosmopolitans-

pretending-that-this-is-an-episode-of-*Sex-in-the-City*-co-workers and tourists wearing their brand new "I Love New York" T-shirts that accentuate their ill-fitting shorts and expensive tennis shoes that they'll probably get knifed over later on in the evening, all grooving to the dulcet tones of REO Speedwagon crooning that they're "gonna keep on loving you."

I *hate* slightly upscale bars in midtown with a 50-50 mix of boring-ass business guys with red faces and navy blue pinstripe suits complaining about their boring-ass "executive decisions of the day" to their younger, female, tipsy-on-five-Cosmopolitans-pretending-that-this-is-an-episode-of-*Sex-in-the-City*-co-workers and tourists wearing their brand new "I Love New York" T-shirts that accentuate their ill-fitting shorts and expensive tennis shoes that they'll probably get knifed over later on in the evening, all grooving to the dulcet tones of REO Speedwagon crooning that they're "gonna keep on loving you."

VERSUS

MUSTANG HARRY'S

352 7TH AVE. BET 29TH AND 30TH STS.
212.268.8930
BEER - AMSTEL LIGHT, $4.00

This is one of those slightly upscale bars in midtown with a 50-50 mix of boring-ass business guys with red faces and navy blue pin-stripe suits complaining about their boring-ass "executive decisions of the day" to their younger, female, tipsy-on-five-Cosmopolitans-pretending-that-this-is-an-episode-of-*Sex-in-the-City*-co-workers and tourists wearing their brand new "I Love New York" T-shirts that accentuate their ill-fitting shorts and expensive tennis shoes that they'll probably get knifed over later on in the evening, all grooving to the dulcet tones of Duran Duran crooning that they're "hungry like the wolf."

I *hate* slightly upscale bars in midtown with a 50-50 mix of boring-ass business guys with red faces and navy blue pinstripe suits complaining about their boring-ass "executive decisions of the day" to their younger, female, tipsy-on-five-Cosmopolitans-pretending-that-this-is-an-episode-of-*Sex-in-the-City*-co-workers and tourists wearing their brand new "I Love New York" T-shirts that accentuate their ill-fitting shorts and expensive tennis shoes that they'll probably get knifed over later on in the evening, all grooving to the dulcet tones of Duran Duran crooning that they're "hungry like the wolf."

AND THE WINNER IS. . .MUSTANG SALLY'S!

Both of these bars are identical, midtown, boring, snoozefest breeding grounds, but if I've got to pick one, I guess I'd rather ride Mustang Sally than Harry.

5:36 P.M. I'm crossing the street at 23rd and 6th and I've got the walk sign, the light is red and this fucking wise-ass cabbie blows his horn at me. It scares the shit out of me. I jump, look at this wild-eyed assface, and he waves me away like I'm in his way. And the light's red. I've got the walk sign. Where's he gonna go? You know? *Where's* he gonna go? So I yell at him, "Where you gonna go?" And he continues to wave me away. Now I'm pissed. This son of a shit-livered prick scares the everloving piss out of me and he's got the balls to keep waving me away like I'm a mosquito pestering him? Well, I'm no mosquito, I'll tell you that much. And the light's red. Where's he gonna go? So this time I slap the hood of the car for emphasis, point to the red light and yell, "Where you gonna go?" And now he's pissed. He's got his head poking out of the window yelling at me in some kooky third-world-country language that sounds like a combination of sub-par yodeling and gibberish. I decide to get out of his way before the light turns green and this transplanted asswipe mows me over. As I walk away I yell once more for good measure,

"Where you gonna go? Asshole!" I don't look back as he yells some third-world insult at me as I walk away. Probably something like, "Your mother unveils her face in public."

You know you're a true New Yorker when you find yourself yelling at a cabbie who probably doesn't speak a lick of English.

PETE'S TAVERN

129 E. 18TH ST. @ IRVING PL.

212.472.7676

BEER - BUDWEISER, $3.50

Pete's Tavern claims to be the oldest original bar in New York City. The tavern opened in 1864 and it retains a certain old-world feeling to this day, with its long black wooden bar and oak booths and tables that line the walls. The whole place has a certain antiqueness to it, and the clientele tend to be staid business types, quietly drinking while chatting in stockbroker-speak, and couples looking for a place to have a quiet drink while playing footsie on their second date.

OVER THE HILL COMES PISSBALL PETE,
FIFTY POUNDS OF SWINGIN' MEAT.

While this isn't known as a young person's hangout, I do remember a Drew Barrymore sighting here a few years ago from "Page Six" in the *Post*. Did you see that *Playboy* issue when Drew did that nude pictorial a few years ago? It was great! All the photos were mind-boggling, but my favorite was one where she was swinging on a tire. And I do mean swinging. She was letting it *all* hang out and I for one was very thankful. I remember staring at that photo and wishing and praying that my name was Goodyear. I think Drew has a perfect body—all pixielike, curvy and boy did she look good nude. And she was *totally* nude. Oh, boy! As a writer, I've learned to be unflinchingly honest, so I'm going to admit that I "used" that issue a lot. Suffice to say it really came in handy—pun fully intended. Sadly, Drew's not here today, but the consolation prize is the fact that there's free popcorn on the bar. It's a little stale, but it's free so I'm eating it. . . .oh, sweet Virginia did Drew look good nude!

VERSUS

PETER'S

182 COLUMBUS AVE. BETWEEN 68TH AND 69TH STS.
212.877.4747
BEER - BUDWEISER, $4.00

Peter's. Pretentious. Preppy. Puke-inducing. Pushy. Painful. Priggish. Pagan. Plutocracy. Pandering. Prattle. Pecuniary. Pitiful. Paltry. Pellucid. Posers. Presumptuous. Pricks. Packed. And at least 50 cell phones in a pear tree. Pleccch.

AND THE WINNER IS. . .PETE'S TAVERN!

They've got free popcorn!

7:15 P.M. As I make my way toward midtown, dripping sweat thanks to the still 90-plus degree weather, I realize I'm starving. I haven't had anything to eat all day, so I decide to stop at a place called Schlotzsky's on the corner of 56th and 6th. As I walk in to what appears to be some sort of fast food/deli type of place with self-serve fountain drinks, pre-packaged salads and cakes and racks of Schlotzsky's own imprinted potato-chip bags dotting the landscape, my gut instincts tell me to flee, but with my stomach growling like a pit bull consumed with wrath, I foolishly head toward the counter where you place your order. As I approach I lock eyes with a young fellow who is manning the counter. He looks like a young Howard Sprague (from the old Andy Griffith show), with a tiny little moustache and spectacles. He's staring straight at me and he's not smiling. His brow is furrowed in what I can only describe as a most curious state. I stare back and approach this unfortunate-looking youth.

"Can I help you?" He asks in a grim tone that one reserves for wakes and funerals, while an understated scowl colors his face.

I scan the menu board behind him and under "sandwiches" I see something listed as the "Original."

"Uh, what's the Original?" I politely ask the young Sprague fellow, hoping he'd lighten up somewhat.

"It's our original sandwich," he answers quickly, blinking his eyes several times in what appears to be a nervous tic.

"Yeah, I figured that," I shoot back with just a hint of sarcasm sneaking into my voice, "but what's *in* it?"

"Oh, um, a couple different kinds of meat, cheese, lettuce, tomatoes, there's other stuff, but that's mainly it," he answers in that same weirdo, Norman Bates-like tone that was starting to really get on my last nerve. His demeanor keeps switching from a thinly veiled look of hate to one of pure and utter fear. And now he's really blinking heavily and it's starting to freak me out. Knowing that this weirdo is probably in close vicinity to knives and other sharp objects that could be used as weapons of destruction, I decide to order and wolf down the food which I so desperately need to keep me going through the night. I briefly weigh the option of walking out, but I wisely decide it might be unsafe to turn my back on this lunatic without ordering something.

"Yeah, alright, I'll take the Original," I say calmly yet firmly. I decide to drop the sarcasm as the kid is now blinking about 80 times per minute.

"You want chips and drink with that?" he queries as he lunges forward while gripping the counter, all the while blinking fast and furious. I notice sweat forming around his tiny brown moustache.

"Yeah, yeah, chips, drink, load me up," I say while forcing a smile. From the looks of the young Howard Sprague, I was coming to the conclusion he was either a psycho, a junkie dying for a fix, or maybe rabies were starting to set in. Perhaps a combination of the three. Whatever, I just wanted to get the sandwich, eat it John Belushi/*Animal House* style and get the hell out of this joint toot sweet. He rang up the total, $6.25, and gave me a receipt that rolled out of the cash register. With ever-blinking eyes and a drop of saliva forming at the left corner of his unsmiling mouth, he tells me to sit down and he'll call the number on my receipt when the food is ready.

I look at the receipt and there's no number on it.

"My receipt doesn't have a number," I point out while holding up my receipt that has a blank spot next to the words, "Your order # is:" The kid's neck stiffens and a vein pops out on his forehead and he tells me through clenched teeth, "Not to worry about it."

So I sit down as the kid hollers out my order to some hapless fool in the back room where they assemble the sandwiches.

After about five uneasy moments the kid announces on the in-store microphone that, "Your Original is ready." He hardly needed the microphone, I'm only about two feet away, but I graciously shrug it off. Let him have his moment of glory. I've learned through years of journalistic duty in the trenches, that when you're faced with a lunatic food vendor, it's best to check your pride at the door.

He seems to have calmed down a little as I take the tray from him, but his blinking eyes are furtively trained on me as I sit down and take a look at my sandwich. And I have to admit this *is* one original sandwich. For starters, the bread is round. It reminds me of a host with a thyroid condition. And when I say host, I'm not talking David Letterman host, I'm talking Catholic religion host. I was brought up Catholic, and in the Catholic mass, in the Communion part, you eat a round piece of bread that symbolizes the body of Jesus Christ. So now as I'm looking at this round bread, I'm having visions of a giant Jesus, clomping around midtown Manhattan like some sort of spiritual King Kong. And I'm not making fun of Jesus Christ or the Catholic religion here, but I'm having scary visions of a giant Jesus for God's sakes. It's like when you take LSD and try not to hallucinate, *that's* when you get the really nasty giant flying spiders and creepy lizards jumping out of lampshades. The more I try to let go of this giant Jesus vision, the more real and frightening it becomes. Put yourself in my shoes. I haven't been to confession in over 25 years, and boy have I sinned a lot in those years. The last thing I need is a giant Jesus chasing me around midtown Manhattan to atone for my many sins.

Trying to ease my mind off this horrible LSD-like flashback, I decide to focus on the inside of the sandwich and forget about the bread. But the insides are almost as frightening as the giant Jesus. There's a mountain of lettuce and onions to make it seem like a whomping big sandwich, but in reality there are only about four thin Oscar Mayer style slices of meat, some sort of yellow Cheez Whiz type cheese and most upsetting and weird, there are black olives in there. Yeah, you read right, black olives. Who in their right minds puts black olives on a sandwich? Nobody, that's who. Black olives should only be brought out at Thanksgiving during the big turkey meal. Those are the rules. And these sick people have just broke this culinary cardinal rule without batting an eye. And speaking of batting eyeballs, I steal a glance at the young Howard Sprague and I see his eyes aren't blinking fast anymore and he's faintly smiling at me. Not once did he tell me that there's black olives in the Original. He fucked me by not warning me about the olives and now he is gloating. The bastard. That fucking sick bastard. Well, to hell with this, I'm not going to take anymore shit, I don't care if the kid is crazier than Richard

Speck with two full-frontal lobotomies, I'm taking a stand, conse-
quences be damned!

I quickly eat the potato chips, have a sip of soda and leave the
sandwich untouched. Then, in full view of the crazy Howard
Sprague kid I take my tray with the uneaten sandwich on top,
head toward the garbage can in the corner and say with all the
sarcasm and cynicism I can dredge up, "The Original. Hah!"
And then with precision-like timing I dump it into the trash in a
sort of way that can only be described as ceremonial. Like I
planned it all along. It's been said that he who laughs last laughs
best, and I can safely say that this much is true.

The smile is quickly erased from the crazy Sprague kid's face
and his eyes are back to the hyperactive blink mode. I see him
reach under the counter and I sense trouble. Quickly I react in
the manner of all trained journalists when faced with danger: I
grab my bag and run out of that place as quick as I can and I
don't look back.

THE 53RD STREET CIGAR BAR

811 7TH AVE. @ 53RD ST.

212.581.1000

BEER - MILLER LITE, $5.36

I guess if you go to a cigar bar, you've got to expect second-hand
cigar smoke, but nothing prepared me for this. It was like walking
face first into Milton Berle's lungs.

As I open the door to this tavern, I'm almost knocked aback
by the Hiroshima-like mushroom cloud of smoke that hangs
heavy in the air. My knees go knobby and my nasal passages
inadvertently shut down. The powerful and almighty cigar stink
was great enough to mask my own sweat-soaked odor, and if you
could smell me, you'd know this is really something to behold, a
real water-to-wine kind of occurrence. Everybody except for me
is puffing on stogies in this small oval-shaped bar which is
attached to the Sheraton Hotel. It's loaded with old-man tourist

types and the short, olive-skinned bartender moves as swiftly as a slug marching through molasses. So after several minutes of breathing in this foul air, I finally get him to bring me a beer. The bar itself is just like your average, boring hotel bar except for the lung-challenging smoke. The only action outside of the constant state of puffery is when one of the old codgers calls someone

on a cell phone and complains about his flight into town that afternoon.

I've smoked cigarettes for over 25 years and even *I* can't handle the smoke in this place. I chug my beer in four minutes flat and vacate quickly, realizing I've probably knocked off at least 30 days of my life sitting in that filthy smoke emporium for ten minutes.

VERSUS

COOPER'S CIGAR BAR

41 W. 58TH ST. BET 5TH AND 6TH AVES.
212.588.8888
BEER - 16 OZ. BUDWEISER (FROM DELI), $1.50

Oh, no. When will it end? For the love of God and country, when will it end? Can you tell me? Can *anyone* tell me? No sense in sugarcoating words, so I'll just tell you plain and simple what's going on here: Cooper's Cigar Bar is closed. It's not open. I repeat, Cooper's Cigar Bar is closed. It's not open.

The sign in the window says, "Coming Soon, Jilly's Piano Bar." Well that's just great. Even if Jilly shows up right this stinking moment and opens up—it's a piano bar. It's not a cigar bar.

THURSDAY

113

It's a goddamned, motherfucking piano bar. Fuck! This was to be a perfect battle of the bars, two cigar bars battling it out amidst cancerous coughs and stink—I wouldn't need to rent a smoke machine, these two bars were going to provide it for free—and now in one fleeting, spirit-crushing moment, that dream is dashed. Gone for good. Over. I have no idea where to find another cigar bar.

Since in addition to my own sweat stink I now reek of cigar smoke, I decide to get a beer from a deli and drink it while hiding in the doorway, much as I did on Sunday as I encountered my first bar flashing the defeating "Closed" sign.

As I'm standing in the locked doorway, drinking my tallboy and looking out for cops while smelling the cigar smoke stench that's imprinted maybe forever in my clothes, I'm tempted to write the words, "Close, but no cigar" in my notes. Luckily good sense intervenes and this moment passes.

You didn't always have to hide in doorways to drink a beer in Manhattan. You used to be able to wander all over this city while drinking beers housed in small brown paper bags. But those days are all over. Take it from me, I served time in stir for the crime of drinking an open beer in this naked city. And now, in lieu of a review for Cooper's Cigar Bar, here for your reading pleasure is my personal true crime story starring myself, a can of beer and two fat cops. . .kids, don't try this outside of your home!

A few years ago, I believe it was 1998, I was walking home and decided to get a beer at a deli. I purchased a 16-ounce can of Budweiser, a man who appeared to be of Indian descent rang it up and placed it in a small, can-sized paper bag. I was traveling down Columbus Avenue and had taken maybe two sips of beer when I heard a police siren howl behind me. Unfazed, I continued to walk. Sirens go off as often as someone with an ass rash changes their underwear, so I didn't think anything of it. But seconds later the police car sidled up to me and a pumped up, young, sporty police officer jumped out and told me to stop.

"Stop what?" I asked this enthusiastic defender of the law.

"What's in the bag?" he asked in a Joe Friday monotone that was a contrast to his boyish face and blond crew cut.

"A can of beer," I candidly answered.

"Sir, do you know that it's against the law to drink open alcohol on the streets?" he quizzed me with ever-narrowing eyes.

"Yeah but this is just a beer," I countered. Somewhere Johnny Cochran was blushing.

"Sir, a beer *is* an alcoholic beverage," he said in clipped tones while folding his arms and shaking his head at my pathetic defense ploy.

"Oh, right," I sheepishly replied. "Well, I'll tell you what, I'll just throw it away and I'll be on my way," I said as I headed toward a garbage can on the street.

"Hold it right there, sir," he commanded. "I'll take the beer. Have you got any I.D.?"

With much sadness I surrendered the beer and watched the sporty cop grin in my direction as he poured it out and then threw the empty can in the street. He must have been out sick the day they teach the young cadets that littering is also against the law. He examined my I.D. and then took out a book of tickets and started writing on the pad.

"Sir, we're doing a sweep of the Upper West Side tonight," he explained in his Joe Friday monotone. "Now, while you think it's no big deal to be drinking a can of beer on the street, this kind of behavior leads people to think it's alright to sit on a stoop and smoke pot. Next thing you know, they're selling crack in broad daylight."

I didn't want to spoil his lecture by informing him that over in the park at 72nd and Broadway they were probably not only selling crack, but mescaline, heroin and all sorts of illegal, mind-altering substances.

"I could've taken you to jail tonight, but I decided to cut you some slack and write you a summons instead. Show up at court on the date instructed and you'll probably be issued a fine." He ripped the ticket off the pad and handed it to me in one fell swoop. Then, with panther-like moves, he jumped into the car. "Stay out of trouble," he warned, jabbing a finger in the air. Then he sped off, probably in hot pursuit of jaywalkers over on Amsterdam and 73rd.

Well, I did what any right-thinking New Yorker would. I pitched the summons in the garbage and bought a six pack of 16-ounce Budweisers and drank them in the safety of my apartment. By all accounts that should've been the end of the story, but let's fast forward to two and a half months later.

I got off work around three in the morning, went home and after many beers I fell asleep somewhere around 5:30 a.m. Roughly 90 minutes later I awoke to a pounding on my door.

"Get the fuck out of here, I'm sleeping!" I gingerly informed this most unwelcome knocker of doors.

And that's when those five horrific words penetrated my eardrums.

"Open up, it's the police!"

I sprang out of bed like a synchronized swimmer jabbed with a cattle prod.

"What?" I mumbled, throwing on a pair of shorts and stumbling to the keyhole on the apartment door.

"Please open your door, this is the police, we have a warrant to pick up Martin Wombacher."

Now my brain was spinning in full hyperactive, hurly-burly mode. This was just too much information to process with a head full of beer and a body functioning on less than two hours of sleep. I peered through the keyhole and spied two potbellied men in their mid-30's wearing baseball caps and T-shirts that were straining under the girth of their guts.

"Is this Martin Wombacher?" one of them asked in a rising voice.

"Yeah, but this must be a mistake, I haven't done anything," I wearily answered.

"Open the door or we'll break it down," the other fatboy threatened.

Fearing the loss of my security deposit, I opened the door.

Fat and fatter burst in and showed me a police warrant with my name on it. They flashed their badges and told me to get dressed and that they were taking me to the holding cell in the precinct jail until the court opens up.

"Jail? Jail? Jail?" I kept repeating this like a mantra. I had no idea why I was being taken to jail, having long forgotten the beer summons.

One of the fatboys took a step toward me.

"Have you been drinking?" he asked as his Silly Putty face twisted into a scowl.

As I looked at the overflowing pile of empty beer cans in the sink and realized that my breath smelled like a floor in the kitchen after a fraternity keg party, I smartly resisted saying, "Duh!"

Instead I retorted with, "I was drinking a couple hours ago, but then I fell asleep. I didn't expect all *this*," I said with a dramatic sweep of the arm. I thought this was a nice touch to punctuate my feelings. The fatboys were unimpressed.

"You like to drink, don't you?" the other one asked. He was slightly taller and he was chewing gum. I assumed he hadn't brought enough for everybody in the room as no offers were made.

"Yeah, I like to drink, so what. Will you please tell me what's going on here?" I asked in a belligerent tone. By now I was awake and was sure this whole thing was some sort of computer glitch. I couldn't wait to throw Officers Fat and Fatter out of my apartment.

The one with the warrant shook the paper in my direction and spoke with one of those "gotcha" smiles.

"Do you remember receiving a ticket for an open beer on Columbus Avenue last August?" he asked while maintaining his goofy-ass grin.

Slowly, through the mist of beer floating in my brain, it came back to me.

"Oh yeah," I replied, as I was becoming stupid with shock. "But you don't mean you're hauling me off to jail over an unpaid ticket for drinking an open can of beer?"

"Bingo," the warrant-holding cop sang out as only a big, fat, warrant-holding cop can sing out. "Mayor Giuliani has instituted a policy where we pick up people with outstanding warrants and take them to court. Since court doesn't open till ten, you're going to have to sit in the holding cell at the precinct.

And that's exactly what happened. The two cops handcuffed me like I was the East Coast Unabomber and drove me to the precinct, where I was processed and thrown into a roughly 12-by-20 foot gray cement jail cell. Luckily it was early and the holding cell was empty except for me and about twenty cockroaches. And we were the *only* things in there. No bench, no cot, nothing but the four grey cement walls, dirty cement floor and a barred window that was about eight feet up on the wall, from where I could hear the cops talking but couldn't see them. After a couple of hours, Fat and Fatter opened the steel door and handcuffed me once again and we drove down to the courthouse. On the way there I was a little concerned because I only had about forty bucks on me. I was sure they were going to slap at least a couple-hundred-dollar fine on me after going to all this trouble.

"I've only got about forty bucks on me," I explained to the fatboys. "Will I be able to go to an ATM machine to get extra money to pay the fine?" I didn't want to have to go back to jail because I couldn't pay the fine.

They grinned knowingly at each other, and the one behind the wheel told me not to worry, that I wouldn't be going back to jail.

When we got to the courthouse on Centre Street the cops led me into the place each holding an arm. The crowd parted like the Red Sea did for Moses, sensing that this handcuffed madman must be some sort of wretched criminal beyond contempt.

Fat and Fatter took the cuffs off once inside the courtroom but had to sit with me until my case was called. Finally, after half an hour, I was called to the bench. I walked up and a guy who looked like the red-haired dweeb from *thirtysomething* introduced himself to me as the public defender.

"How do you wish to plead, Martin?" he asked.

"Guilty, let's just get this thing over with," I hurriedly shot back. I always hated the show *thirtysomething* and was pissed that the one time I get a public defender, he has to look like that red-haired goofus.

"You spent the morning in jail, right Martin?" he asked.

"Yeah," I answered as I looked up and saw the judge for the first time. He was old, bald and looked as hungover as I was. I sensed he just wanted to get this thing over as much as I did.

"Your Honor," *thirtysomething* said as he turned toward the uninterested Judge, "the defendant wishes to enter a guilty plea. In light of the fact that he spent the morning in jail, I suggest that the court reduce the fine to $30.

I just remember standing there thinking, "$30?"

Then I heard the gavel hit. . .well, whatever the gavel hits, and the judge instructed me to pay the clerk.

I looked at *thirtysomething* and said, "Thirty dollars? That's it?"

"Yeah, the clerk is right down the hall, you can pay there, show them this," he instructed, handing me some paperwork.

"Thirty dollars?" I repeated again. I felt like I had been raped and then fist-fucked. I went through probably the shittiest and weirdest morning of my life and all for a stinking 30 bucks?

"You've got to be kidding me," I said to *thirtysomething*.

With this the next case was called and the public defender told me once again to go to the clerk's office. They had to make room for the next case.

Feeling shattered, I started down the hall to the clerk's office. On the way I passed Fat and Fatter. They waved as they passed by and they were laughing.

And I know why. This city humiliated me, and they thought it was funny. They were laughing at me. It was like I was Jesus and after carrying the cross for miles nobody bothers to nail you up on the fucking thing. Thirty bucks. . .shit. I mean, at least slap me with some humongous fine to make this whole charade seem worth *something*. Thirty bucks wouldn't even cover the city's expenses. It just didn't make any sense, and sense was the one thing I needed on that horrible, stinking, rotten morning. No, I had been rat-fucked and there was nothing I could do about it.

Just like there's nothing I can do now about the closing of Cooper's Cigar Bar. Except drink this beer in paranoid silence while keeping my eyes peeled for Johnny Law.

AND THE WINNER IS. . .COOPER'S CIGAR BAR!

Because it was closed, probably adding at least half an hour to this writer's life.

9:17 P.M. I'm on the subway heading downtown, and sitting directly across from me is an old woman, at least 80 years old, and she keeps quarter-folding her newspaper with her bony, age-mangled hands, then unquartering it, then repeating the whole process, all the while saying, "Shit. . .shit. . .shit. . . ." It's quite mesmerizing and I'm very happy to have witnessed this unique brand of lunacy. I have nothing more to add. Carry on, tally ho and hip, hip hooray.

FLIGHT 151

151 8TH AVE. BETWEEN 17TH AND 18TH STS.
212.229.1868
BEER - HEINEKEN, $5.00

This bar is named Flight 151, and I think it's supposed to be fashioned to resemble an airplane hangar. Coffee, tea or beer? There's a neon airplane on the wall and a few other flight-related decorations here and there, but to me it resembles something else. A neighborhood bar. Plain and simple. And not that there's anything wrong with that. There are different drink specials every night and the crowd is mainly neighborhood locals. There are

IT'S A BIRD, IT'S A PLANE, IT'S. . .IT'S. . .A BOTTLE OF HEINEKEN.

THURSDAY

booths and tables if you want to sit down and eat a meal, and there are crayons on the tables if you want to draw a picture on the white paper tablecloth and take it to Iggy's Kick Ass Bar. The waitresses are friendly, and those two words that always bring a smile to this bar reviewer's face are evident here. . .no, it's not *heaving breasts,* it's: *Free popcorn!*

VERSUS

FLIGHT 1668

1668 3RD AVE. BETWEEN 93RD AND 94TH STS.

212.426.1416

BEER - BUDWEISER, $3.00

I feel like a fool. I thought I had really found something great when I discovered that there were two bars in Manhattan starting out with "Flight" in the name. I was figuring I could do some kind of goof on Cindy Adams' tagline, "Only in New York kids, only in New York." I had all kinds of ideas brewing in my brain. One of them was to have the bartenders here badmouth Flight 151. Then I thought I'd go back and tell 151 and maybe get a real fight brewing here. This was going to be great! So imagine how I feel as I walk in, order a beer and say to the bartender, "You know there's a bar downtown called Flight 151."

That's when the bartender hits me between the eyes with this flying mallet of a statement: "Yeah, I know, we've got the same owner."

I should've known. I should've checked. Jesus, have I got my head up my ass! Well, that shoots *this* battle to shit. They're not going to dish dirt on each other if they're owned by the same people. . . .Jesus, have I got my head up my ass!

AND THE WINNER IS. . .AWW, WHO CARES!

Jesus, have I got my head up my ass!

10:45 P.M. Maybe I should've eaten that stupid-ass Original. My stomach is starting to knot up and now I'm afraid to eat for fear I'll throw up. Luckily I've got over half a roll of Rolaids in my pocket. I'll snack on them on the way to the next joint. I still can't believe those sick fuckers put black olives on a sandwich!

BARCOASTAL (FORMERLY THE COWBOY BAR)

1495 1ST AVE. @ 78TH ST.

212.288.6635

BEER - BUDWEISER, $4.00

Well, here's a new problem. The Cowboy Bar is open, but they changed their name to Barcoastal. Get it? *Barcoastal.* Woops, neither do I.

VERSUS

COWGIRL HALL OF FAME

519 HUDSON ST. @ 10TH ST.

212.633.1133

BEER - BUDWEISER, $3.50

This is a cutesy-wootsy, cowgirl/southern themed bar in the West Village. Some of the staff wear cowboy hats and some do not. There's kitschy cowgirl/cowboy decorations plastered here, there and everywhere. This

THURSDAY

place specializes in margaritas, but I'm drinking beer, so that's of no consequence to me. As I sit here I get the distinct feeling that this place would be more at home in Disneyland, next to the Country Bear Jamboree. I've got bad memories of the Country Bear Jamboree, so I'm never coming here again. You can do what you want, but don't say I didn't warn you.

AND THE WINNER IS. . .COWGIRL HALL OF FAME!

Barcoastal. . .*Barcoastal?*

12:25 A.M. Okay, so here's my Country Bear Jamboree story. When I was a senior in high school, about ten of us piled into two beat-up cars and drove to Florida. One of the stops on the trip was Disneyland or Disneyworld, whichever one of those is in Florida, I can never remember. Anyway, we all take acid before we go to Disneyland and once we're there we split up into groups of two to roam around Walt's world while tripping our brains' fantastic. I end up pairing up with my friend Dan, who up to this point had never touched any type of strong drugs. He'd drawn the line for years at beer and pot and now he decides to take a whopping dose of acid in the land of giant Mickey Mouses and Goofys. I thought it would be hilarious, so I told him I'd keep an eye on him. Well, the acid kicks in and Dan's freaking out. Everything's scaring him and he's freaking out and he appears to be frightening small children. So I decide the best thing would be to go to the Country Bear Jamboree. I figure this will cool him out and then maybe he'd start having fun like I was. The only difference was I had been eating acid for breakfast for the last two years, so this is literally a walk in the park for me. A walk in a theme park, but a walk in the park all the same. Well, we manage to get into our seats okay, but seconds after we sit down, Dan grabs my arm so tight I think he's going to break it in half. I look at his face and it's pure white, all the blood is drained out of it. I thought maybe he was having a heart attack and now *I'm* freaking out.

"You okay? Can you breathe?" I ask him. He doesn't answer, he just keeps staring upward. "What the fuck is wrong with you?" I yell at him while forcing his hand off my arm and the family in front of us to leave.

"Do you see that bear up there?" Dan asks while pointing to a fake bear head that was one of many that lined the ceiling.

"Yeah, I see it," I answer, trying to figure out what he was talking about.

"Well, he's been staring at me since we sat down!" he answered as complete terror colored his face and a tear welled up in his eye.

He didn't fare much better on Mr. Toad's Wild Ride. Somewhere in the course of the day I lost track of Dan and I found him hours later in a store where he had purchased over $75 worth of Mickey Mouse dolls. It took me half an hour to convince the clerk to give him back his money.

BILL'S GAY NINETIES

57 E. 54TH ST. BETWEEN MADISON AND PARK AVES.

212.355.0243

BEER - BUDWEISER, $4.00

Sure, you could mention the turn-of-the-century ambience in Bill's. Maybe throw in something about the framed photos of the jockeys and racing horses that line the dark, wooden walls from that era. Maybe throw in a sentence or two about the free live music. Of course you'd want to mention that the clientele is a lively crowd that is a mixture of locals and tourists. But in the long run, one word sums up this midtown tavern, and that word is: *Gay!*

VERSUS

THE COCK

188 AVE. A @ 12TH ST.

212.946.1871

BEER - BUDWEISER, $4.00

Well now, this is a pleasant surprise. I was expecting this to be yet another theme bar with all kinds of Rooster knickknacks plastered to and fro. Instead, DJ's are playing a combination of '80s music and funk classics. It's crowded in here. It's mainly all men and they are quite friendly fellows. They're *really* friendly. In fact, they're dancing with each other and. . .oh. . .they mean *that* kind of cock.

AND THE WINNER IS. . .THE COCK!

Old Bill may be the gayest in the land, but you know it's gotta be hard to beat the Cock.

1:50 A.M. Her breasts were *heaving*, goddammit!

THURSDAY

BLEECKER ST. BARS

FEATURING THE PSYCHIC WHO COULDN'T SPELL STRAIGHT AND RECIPES FROM INSANE MURDERERS

12:05 P.M. Yesterday's scattered, all-over-the-city bar battles have left me fatigued, and a true General Patton-like weariness has sunk into my battered body. My head aches, my eyes are reduced to sunken globes of a pinkish hue and my jeans stink of blood, sweat and beers. Today will be a more relaxed day as I plan to keep close to home by leisurely reviewing bars on Bleecker Street, a mere pebble's throw away.

The reason I chose Bleecker Street, other than the fact that it's close by, is because in my wild-eyed youth, when I was in high school in the midwest town of Peoria, Illinois, my friends and I would pile in a couple of cars and park in a field on the outskirts of town where we'd proceed to get high on a variety of pills, powders, smoke and beer. When it was winter we'd sit in the beat-up cars with the heaters on like they were our little apartments, stoned out of our gourds, jabbering, joking and being silly in a carefree way only a stoned 16-year-old can be. When it was an exceptionally clear night we tuned up and down the FM dial for a late-night show called "Bleecker Street." The DJ/emcee of the Bleecker Street show was one of those low-voiced, stoned/smooth-talking DJ's who emanated "cool" in the mid-'70s. He'd play music unknown and unheard of in Peoria, Illinois—the first time I ever heard the Velvet Underground was on "Bleecker Street"—and we'd get high, drink and listen intently to these new and wonderful sounds. We all wondered where this elusive Bleecker Street was until one night the stoned DJ announced, "You're listening to Bleecker Street, here in New York City, maaan." I remember trying to imagine what Bleecker Street and New York were like. Even my imagination stoked to the gills on pot, various pills and cheap cans of Blatz beer failed to conjure up the proper imagery, but I knew it was worlds away from sitting in a car in the middle of a field, stoned to the bone in Peoria, Illinois.

Most of the people I used to sit in cars and get high and drink cheap beer with are still in Peoria. The majority of them are married with kids, cars, square jobs, house payments and lives steeped in the middle-class world of midwest America. And as I consider my life of freelance writing, being single, working a goofy, responsibility-free night-shift job to pay my rent in New York City while I count the 56 bucks in my only pair of jeans, gather up my cigarettes and head out the door to drink 14 beers in 14 bars on Bleecker Street, I feel like the luckiest son of a bitch in the land.

1:15 P.M. The raging, burning, inferno-like temperature has somewhat let up today. Instead of hellish 100-degree weather, it's in the vicinity of a somewhat more Purgatory-like low-90's kind of day. Although as I walk down 6th Avenue, rings of sweat are already growing in the nether regions of my underarm area. And the rash. . .well, never mind.

I stop at a deli between 14th and 15th Streets for a Diet Mountain Dew caffeine pick-me-up, and I'm looking across the street at a building with a garish purple/brown awning on the second floor advertising a "Psichic Gallery with Tarot Cards and Palm Readings." As I look in my almost empty, lime-green 16-ounce plastic bottle of Mountain Dew, I see a vision. . .it's getting clearer. . .I see something in the future for this "Psichic" . . .it's almost visible now. . .and here it is. . .it's. . .it's. . .a spelling lesson!

1:29 P.M. I'm walking up the stairs to visit the psychic who can't spell straight. I was drawn to this place the minute after reading the spelling-challenged sign. There's something irresistible about meeting a soothsayer who can peer into the future, but has difficulty putting letters in the right formation to list her own chosen occupation.

As I reach the second floor I spy a nameplate on the door with the name of Anne Marie. It's the only door on the floor, so this must be the place. But I thought the psychic who couldn't spell straight would have a somewhat more exotic name. Something like Shayaliah, Kasliamandi or Geraldo at the very least, but Ann Marie? To me Ann Marie sounds more like a baker of cookies or perhaps a June Taylor Dancer than a psychic. Of course, with her inept spelling skills maybe Ann Marie *is* the way she spells Geraldo. I decide to give her the benefit of the doubt and ring the bell. But nothing happens when I press the button; there's no ringing. I stand there and realize that since she's a psychic, she probably disconnected the distracting bell, because she already knows I'm here. She must be very, *very* good.

1:35 P.M. Maybe she's not that good. I've been standing here for close to five minutes and no one's opened the door. So I proceed to rap on the black, wooden door and it slowly opens up about six inches. I'm now eyeball to eyeball with part of a woman's face staring back at me. She doesn't speak, so I make the first move.

"Hi, are you. . .the. . .uh. . .psychic?" I ask as I notice a certain amount of nervousness creeping into my voice. I'm realizing I've never spoken to a psychic and all of the sudden I've got these

MAYBE THEY SHOULD SPEND LESS TIME LOOKING INTO THE FUTURE AND A LITTLE MORE TIME CHECKING OUT A LITTLE THING WE LIKE TO CALL "THE DICTIONARY."

weird, first-date kind of butterflies swooping around in my stomach.

The door opens up as she answers, "Yes, I'm Ann. Would you like a reading?"

Well, of course I have to answer in the affirmative at this point; what am I supposed to say, "No, I just thought I'd drop by and give you the proper spelling for *psychic?*" Nope, I'm locked into this thing now with no hope for retreat, and besides, I find myself strangely attracted to Ann Marie. I would guess her to be in her early to mid twenties, she's wearing a loose green sweater, a blue jean skirt, her light brown hair is down around her shoulders and she's got these big, droopy, dreamy eyes. Maybe it's just me, but I'm picking up this vibe around her like she'd really be into. . .well, you know. . .*weird* stuff. You know, candle wax, whipped cream, handcuffs, *The Jetsons.* I'm trying to avoid having some sort of mental sexual fantasy, seeing that she's a psychic and maybe is reading my thoughts right now, but just like when someone tells you not to think of a certain subject, I just can't stop myself.

As I follow her into the apartment, we stroll into a large main room where there's a square table with two wooden chairs on either side of it along with some Jesus statues by the window. I'm assuming this is where the reading will be done. So I sit down in one of the chairs. Just then my *Penthouse* Forum-like fantasy of Ann Marie licking my palm while reading it is shattered by her saying, "I'm over here, this is where we do it."

Before I even look over, I'm processing the words, "This is where we do it." Oh, my. Seconds later I look over to a corner of the room and Ann Marie is seated in a tiny little nook in the wall that has a light green cloth curtain attached to the entrance.

"Oh, you do the reading in there?" I sheepishly ask.

"Please come," she says, waving me over.

"Please come? Sweet mother of George Jetson!" I'm thinking to myself as I walk into this tiny little room. Once inside she draws the green curtain and I sit down in a chair next to a tiny little glass-top covered table. Three plastic Jesus statues and a large, unlit, 99-cent-store-quality yellow candle decorate the table. Ann Marie is talking but I'm not listening because as I look down I see her blue jean skirt is slit up above her knees and I'm now staring at her kneecaps and they're really nice. I really like kneecaps and Ann Marie is blessed with a couple of beauties. Sturdy yet soft at the same time. I'm brought back to earth as she coughs and says, "So what will it be?"

I didn't want her to know so early into our relationship that I wasn't listening because of my kneecap fetish so, remembering the information from the infamous "Psichic" awning, I say, "What about the tarot cards?"

"That's $25 for a complete reading," she tells me. I notice she never smiles or shows much emotion, and that of course is a major turn on.

"Okay, let's do it," I say, getting into the spirit of Ann Marie's sexual double entendres.

"I'll get the cards," she replies in her emotionless, somewhat monotone voice.

For some reason I was sure she'd be nude when she returned. I'd light the candle and pretty soon we'd both be sprawling on the floor barking in unison like two Astros in heat. Sadly, this wasn't to be the case.

She came back fully clothed holding a colorful deck of oversized cards and placed them on the table. As she sat down, she took the material where the skirt was slit and covered up her kneecaps. What a gyp! Then she told me to shuffle the cards.

I picked them up and half-heartedly shuffled them around in my hands as I was still reeling from the kneecap cover-up.

"That's it," Ann Marie teasingly said as I shuffled. I looked down to see her kneecaps were once again visible. If her intent was to tease me, she was doing a bang-up job. She took the cards from my hands and told me to pick out 17.

Keeping one eye on the kneecaps and one on the cards, I successfully picked out 17 cards.

"Put them on the table," Ann Marie instructed.

I did so with a confident sweep of the hand and a cock of the right eyebrow in her direction.

She picked up the cards and swiftly dealt them on the table in different formations and started explaining what they meant. We locked eyes as she told me I had a long life span and that I'd probably make it to 87 years old. I didn't have the heart to tell her my doctor recently told me if I don't cut down on my drinking and smoking, I'd be lucky to see 50. She said she saw great success in my future and that a former lover in my life is coming back.

"For what?" I wondered silently to myself, running through a list of luckless women who have bounded in and out of my life, spanning from my ex-wife from the early '80s to girlfriends from the last two decades. I came to the steadfast conclusion that if any of them come back with the sorrowful intention of borrowing money, they're shit out of luck.

She spewed out some more generic fortune-cookie-type forecasts for my future, but my focus was locked back on her kneecaps, for now instead of covering them up, she adjusted in her chair and actually lifted her skirt higher. In my mind the words "Jane his wife" sang out loud and clear.

"Do you have any questions you'd like to ask me?" Ann Marie

asked as I was dropping off into full-bore kneecap fantasy.

I sat there pondering this for a full minute. "Maybe I should ask something dirty to get the ball rolling," I thought to myself. As usual I chickened out.

"Umm. . .well, it's a little personal," I said, once again locking eyeballs with the lovely Ann Marie.

She was unfazed. "That's okay. Just think of the question in your mind and pick three cards. Maybe I can answer without you asking the question."

As I picked three cards I mentally asked the question, "Can I suck your kneecaps?"

Anne Marie looked puzzled as she studied the cards.

All the while I'm sitting there thinking, "Well, can I or can't I?"

Ann Marie frowned. I feared her kneecaps were off territory.

"I'm going to be honest with you," she said while pointing to the tarot cards, "I can't make any sense of these cards. If you want the answer, it's best if you ask me the question."

This is it, do or die time. This is the mark of a *real* man's man. I would either ask the kneecap question and take the chance of her either being into it or slapping me or maybe even calling the cops, or wuss out and ask a fake question and have to stoop to handing it to myself while studying my tattered nude Drew Barrymore copy of *Playboy* later on. I took a deep breath, waited 10 seconds, exhaled and asked, "Uh. . .I'm working on a book and I was wondering if after the New Year would be a good time to try and promote it?"

The lovely Ann Marie said it would be and walked me to the door, and said goodbye. As I walked down the stairs I thanked God for Drew Barrymore and *Playboy*.

CBGB's 313 Gallery

313 Bowery @ Bleecker St.

212.982.4052

Beer - Heineken, $5.50

I was going to have a beer at CBGB next door, but it's not open yet, so I opted to have one at CB's sister bar. This is the quieter version of CBGB, especially at three in the afternoon. I'm the only one at the bar, except for the young female bartender with blonde streaks in her punky hairdo and her vintage 1988 Van Halen concert T-shirt. The bar has kind of a cafe-like feel to it with artwork on the walls and chairs and tables leading up to the stage. If you come here at night you can leave the ear plugs at home. The music featured here is usually more of an "Unplugged" folksy-type quality, in stark contrast to the original CBGB's punk and thrash fare. As I sip my beer I notice that behind the bar they have more than 16 different types of CBGB T-shirts for sale, just like it's the freaking Hard Rock Cafe. Wait a second, what's that noise? Oh, it's Joey Ramone throwing up in heaven.

3:30 P.M. As I cross the corner of Bleecker and Bowery I see what appears to be a homeless man in tattered clothing picking through the trash. And he's wearing a pair of red suede shoes. This is a first for me; I've never seen a homeless person wearing red shoes while diligently picking through garbage. I'm quite perplexed by this sighting until three words pop into my mind: "Michael Musto's trash."

VON

3 Bleecker St. between Bowery and Layfayette St.
212.473.3039
Beer - Budweiser, $4.00

Von is a small bar that's dark even in the light of day. It's slightly upscale and the clientele appear to be somewhat artsy fartsy, young college kids who will probably be CEOs of their fathers' companies in 10 years time. Reggae music is playing and a big Marmaduke dog roams freely around the bar. Like, groovy, huh?

There's a young, goateed hipster sitting two bar stools to my left, and I hear him say to his horn-rimmed-glasses-wearing girlfriend who probably doesn't even need glasses, "Smoking is a really deep thing, man." I fight the urge to throw up in their matching Cosmopolitan drinks that they'll probably nurse for an hour and then stiff the bartender out of a tip as they leave to attend their yoga class.

And the last comment I have about this bar is: Who in the fuck names a bar Von? I mean, I'd feel like a real first-class jackoff saying to someone, "Let's meet at Von tonight."

Who wants to say that? What's that all about? Von?. . .Von?

4:00 P.M. Von?

BLEECKER STREET BAR

58 BLEECKER ST. @ CROSBY ST.

212.334.0244

BEER - RED STRIPE, $4.50

Pretty much your standard NYU type of college bar with a classic-rock jukebox. "Benny, Benny, Benny and the Jets." A couple of pool tables in the back. "Benny, Benny, Benny and the Jets." Neighborhood locals and a biker or two at the bar. "Benny, Benny, Benny and the Jets." Two girls sitting at a table talking into  cell phones. "Benny, Benny, Benny and the Jets." Fake vintage beer signs. "Benny, Benny, Benny and the Jets." Oh, but it's weird and it's wonderful. Okay, it's not that weird and calling it wonderful *is* a bit of a stretch, but at least it's not named *Von*.

4:27 P.M. Von?

VG BAR

643 BROADWAY @ BLEECKER ST.

NO PHONE LISTING

BEER - BUDWEISER, $4.00

Remember the show *Archie's Place*? You remember, the sequel to *All in the Family* where Archie owned a saloon in Queens? Well, this small, square-shaped bar reminds me of *Archie's Place*, but with new furniture. Remember how boring *Archie's Place* was? Well. . .ditto.

5:05 P.M. I stop at a deli across the street from the VG bar to get a new pack of cigarettes and they have a radio that's tuned to some MOR rock station. I cough up $5.25 for a pack of Camel Lights while Rod Stewart is crooning, "Tonight I'm yours, do anything that you want me to. Don't hurt me, don't hurt me." And I'm wondering, how could a woman hurt this preening rock star? I mean his hair's already all mussed up and everything. As I walk out of the deli I come to the conclusion that sometime in the future, Rod Stewart could be to delis what Phil Collins is to Rite Aids. Granted this is just pure speculation on my part, but I think that time will indeed be on my side and prove me right. That's what I think.

SEÑOR SWANKY'S

142 BLEECKER ST. @ LAGUARDIA PL.

212.979.9800

BEER - ROLLING ROCK, $5.00

The subtitle to Señor Swanky's is "Mexican Cafe and Celebrity Hangout." But as I stroll into this faux Mexican bar decorated with cheap sombreros hanging over the bar and wicker bar stools that would be more at home in a Tiki bar, the closest thing

TOURISTS OR TOURISTAS? YOU DECIDE.

to a celebrity I see is a hagged-out, old broad with bottle-blonde hair, way too much makeup and fake tits who resembles Pamela Anderson in a way that could only be described as cruel. And the gentleman she's drinking margaritas with could *maybe* pass for an aged James Brolin with severe liver disease. Just maybe.

Unbelievably they charge $5 for a bottle of Rolling Rock, and there's no free chips and salsa on the bar. That's the one saving grace of a Mexican bar, there's *always* free food. But not here. They do have matches on the bar though, and the copy on the matchbook reads as follows: "The Place Where People Who Know People, Who Know People, Who Know Nobody, Go to Eat & Drink." Uh. . .could you repeat that? On second thought, please don't.

La Margarita

184 Thompson St. @ Bleecker St.
Phone: 212.533.2410
Beer - Budweiser, $4.00

This place is yet another standard Mexican restaurant/bar that's right down the block from Señor Swanky's, but one accoutrement makes it seems worlds away. Yes, that's right, free chips and salsa! Hallelujah.

Donde, est strehlo. Est anderle sous de la mucho same-same. Hasta la chips de freebee!

6:20 P.M. It's kind of rough writing travelogue pieces when I'm basically walking down the same street, sometimes only a half a block, to the next bar. So I've decided that in times when nothing interesting in my travels is happening I'll insert an entry from my collection of recipes from insane murderers for your reading and culinary pleasure. Here's the first one. Bon apetit!

TED BUNDY'S CREAMY LIVER WITH ONIONS

1 1/2   *pounds calves or baby beef liver, cut into 1-inch strips*
1/2   *teaspoon salt*
1/8   *teaspoon pepper*
1/4   *cup butter*
2   *onions thinly sliced*
1   *8-ounce can sliced mushrooms, undrained*
2   *cups dairy sour cream*
1   *teaspoon Worcestershire sauce*

1. Season liver with salt and pepper. Preheat skillet, uncovered, at 325 degrees. Melt butter and saute onions until tender. Add liver and brown on all sides.

2. Add mushrooms with liquid. Reduce heat to simmer. Simmer, covered for 8 to 10 minutes.

3. Add sour cream and continue cooking for an additional 8 to 10 minutes. Add Worcestershire sauce. Makes 6 servings.

PECULIER PUB

145 BLEECKER ST. BETWEEN LAGUARDIA PL.
AND THOMPSON ST.
212.353.1327
BEER - BUDWEISER, $3.50

Looking for a bit of strange? Then this is your place. There's 450 different varieties of bottled beer to be had here from more than

45 different countries. The bar atmosphere has a large, German beerhouse feel to it with its emphasis on large wooden booths and an atmosphere that literally screams, "Hogan!" The clientele is a 50/50 mix of NYU kids and beery-eyed locals traveling around the world on 450 beers.

6:55 P.M.

JOHN WAYNE GACY'S HOLIDAY PINEAPPLE-GLAZED HAM SLICE

1	smoked ham slice, 1-inch thick
3/4	cup orange juice
1/4	cup brown sugar
4	pineapple slices

1. Preheat skillet, uncovered, at 325 degrees. Cook ham until lightly browned on both sides for 8 to 10 minutes per side. Remove from skillet and keep hot.

2. Combine orange juice and brown sugar in skillet. Bring to a boil at 225 degrees. Add pineapple slices and glaze fruit.

3. Arrange fruit on top of ham. Pour orange sauce over ham and serve at once. Makes 3 to 4 servings.

FRIDAY

THE BITTER END

147 BLEECKER ST. BETWEEN LAGUARDIA PL.
AND THOMPSON ST.
212.673.7030
BEER - BUDWEISER, $3.50

This no frills, legendary folky bar has been in operation since 1962. Isn't it about time someone put it out of its misery? Billy Joel, Fred Neil, Joni Mitchell and Neil Young have all played here in the past. But now that it's the present, they don't come near this dump.

7:20 P.M.

RICHARD SPECK'S RED, WHITE AND BLUE AMERICAN FRIED POTATOES

For each serving:

- 1   *medium potato*
- 1   *tablespoon butter or margarine*
- 1/2   *teaspoon salt*
- 1/8   *teaspoon pepper*

1. Pare at least 4 potatoes; slice thin. Rinse with cold water and pat dry. Season as desired.

2. Preheat skillet, uncovered, at 325 degrees. Melt butter or margarine. Spread potatoes evenly in skillet.

3. Cover, with vent open, and fry 15 minutes. Uncover, turn potatoes and season with salt and pepper. Fry, uncovered, for 15 minutes, loosening potatoes occasionally.

4. Garnish dish with a tiny American flag for a Fourth of July treat.

FRIDAY

KENNY'S CASTAWAYS

157 BLEECKER ST. BETWEEN THOMPSON AND SULLIVAN STS.

212.979.9762

BEER - BUDWEISER, $3.00

Kenny's Castaways is probably the only place where rock and roll music and the words, "just say no" are comfortably housed together. At Kenny's there's no happy hour, no drink specials, no food, and no frills. They do, however, claim to have the cheapest daytime drink prices on Bleecker Street (you can negotiate with the bartender) and live music seven nights a week. The bands range from Led Zeppelin cover bands to Nirvana wannabes performing their original tunes. There's also an eclectic jukebox featuring CD's from *Sgt. Pepper* to The Popsicles.

Behind the 32-foot wooden bar there are 14 beers on tap including Sam Adams, Guinness and Bass ale, all priced in the four-dollar range. The most expensive drink is a Long Island Iced Tea at $7.00. The garage band/frathouse atmosphere includes a stuffed deer head on the wall, Elvis lamps, and a "V.I.P." bar and tables upstairs that's open on Friday and Saturday nights. In summation: A three hour tour. . .a three hour tour.

KENNY'S LITTLE CREATURES ON DISPLAY.

7:20 P.M. I'm halfway between Thompson and Sullivan Streets when I look up and see the sign, "Suzie's Finest Chinese Cuisine."

"Suzie's finest chinese cuisine," I mumble to myself, rolling the words around in my mouth just to see how it feels to actually utter such a bold and totally confident statement. Seconds later I was being seated at a table by a small Chinese man while another put a silver pot of tea on my small, square wooden table. A third man approached with a glass filled with ice and water. He also had a large menu which was colored blood red. He handed it to me with a quick, whipstart wave of the wrist.

And then the men disappeared and I sat alone at my table staring at the menu, the silver tea pot and the glass filled with ice and water. It's precisely at this moment, while staring at the ice floating in the cool, clear water that my mind starts swimming upstream like so much summer salmon. Thoughts skip into my brain of muted lightning on the Fourth of July, a flower that's blooming in a field just north of Des Moines, Iowa, porpoises mating in unchartered waters, fine woolen socks, the possessive form of a sidewalk, soft broad-brimmed hats, a shrunken nose that has begun to grow again, a piece of music composed for two performers, black-and-white coloring books, biological organisms created in laboratories, volcanoes erupting molten ash, a man making a mirror just to see himself, ten rows of sleeping babies, a ringing golden bell, well-worn copies of *The Farmer's Almanac*, warm mashed potatoes on a winter night, a deceased person who becomes a saint, uncontrollable urges to gamble, astronomical research by satellites, invisible sheets of ice, territories of continual international controversy, a chocolate layer cake, a vague term that expresses abstract art, a small pile of sparkling knitting needles, one number past a dozen, a sugary fluid in a plastic yellow glass, economic systems governed by paper currency, thoughts surrendering to a void, it is shining. . .it is shining.

I had a bowl of hot and sour soup, wontons in hot sesame sauce and steamed shrimp dumplings. Was it the *finest* Chinese cuisine to be had in this man's world? I don't know if I'm qualified to surrender such a conclusion, but it *was* pretty fucking good.

THE BACK FENCE

155 BLEECKER ST. @ THOMPSON ST.
212.475.9221
BEER - BUDWEISER, $3.00

The Back Fence has been a fixture on Bleecker Street for over 35 years. There's live rock and roll played here every night and it attracts an eclectic crowd of bikers, old hippies, college kids and tourists. The floor is covered with sawdust and shells from the free peanuts on the bar and the decor is rustic wooden fences. Buyer beware though: Sundays they feature an open mic poetry session. BYOB (bring your own bongos).

8:45 P.M.

ERIC HARRIS AND DYLAN KLEBOLD'S BAKED APPLE BONANZA

6 to 8   *apples, cored*
1/4   *cup raisins*
1/4   *cup chopped nuts*
3   *tablespoons butter or margarine*
1   *cup brown sugar*
1/2   *cup cinnamon*
1   *cup water*

1. Remove 1-inch peel around top of each cored apple. Place apples in skillet. Fill each center with combined raisin and nut mixture; dot with butter or margarine.

2. Combine sugar and cinnamon. Sprinkle over apples. Add water to skillet. Cover at 300 degrees and bring water to boil.

3. Reduce heat to simmer. Cook apples until tender for 30 to 35 minutes. Baste with syrup occasionally. Makes 6 to 8 servings.

VILLAGE LANTERN

167 BLEECKER ST. @ SULLIVAN ST.
212.260.7993
BEER - BUDWEISER, $3.75

This is an upscale bar with brick walls and candles burning everywhere. There's an additional room downstairs with tables and a stage, but it's empty tonight. I'm assuming they have live music, but don't quote me because I'm too tired to ask the bartender. It's quiet in here with jazz music piped in, and most everybody in the joint appears to be on a first or second date. Except for me, all alone staring into my beer while visions of Ann Marie's kneecaps dance in my beer-soaked mind. Sigh.

ARTHUR'S TAVERN

57 GROVE ST. BETWEEN BLEECKER ST. AND 7TH AVE.
212.675.6879
BEER - BUDWEISER, $3.00

In the theme song to the movie *Arthur*, Christopher Cross sings, "When you get lost between the moon and New York City, the best that you can do is fall in love." I have never, ever understood

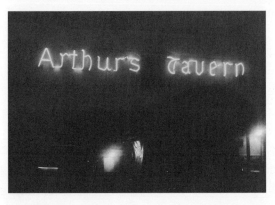

those lyrics. Can someone please explain to me *who* is getting lost between the moon and New York City? I've lived here for over eight years and I'll be damned if I've ever come across any moon travelers. Much less, direction-challenged moon travelers. I've heard thousands of conversations in restaurants, bars, subways and work and none of them have ever begun with, "What a week this has been, first I got lost between the moon and New York City and then. . ." I've never heard that conversation, have you? I didn't think so. Christopher Cross, what an ass!

Oh, I almost forgot the review. Arthur's Tavern is this small little club with Christmas decorations and lights even in summer and live jazz. Yeeha.

10:15 P.M.

ED GEIN'S GLORI-FRIED CHOPS

4 to 6 pork chops, 1/2 inch thick
1 teaspoon salt
1 teaspoon pepper
1 10 1/2-ounce can condensed cream of mushroom or celery soup

1. Preheat skillet, uncovered, at 325 degrees. Brown chops for 5 minutes per side. Season chops with salt and pepper.

2. Cover chops with soup. Reduce heat to simmer. Cover and simmer for 15 to 20 minutes or until fork tender. Reduce heat to warm for serving. Makes 4 to 6 servings.

JEKYLL & HYDE

91 7TH AVE. S. BETWEEN BLEECKER

AND CHRISTOPHER STS.

212.989.7701

BEER - BUDWEISER, $4.00

And now, once again, I present my patent-pending, standing theme bar/restaurant review: "See Cafe, Hard Rock."

11:20 P.M.

CHARLIE MANSON'S
CHEEZ WHIZ ON CRACKERS

20 *saltine crackers*
 1 *jar of Cheez Whiz*

1. Spread Cheez Whiz evenly on every cracker.
2. Place on tray, serve to family members and enjoy.

COMOLLO'S

359 6TH AVE. @ WASHINGTON PL.

212.243.9782

BEER - BUDWEISER, $3.50

As I veer away from Bleecker Street heading homeward, my last stop is this small, dimly lit, lounge-like bar/restaurant. I'm the only one in here except for the bartender. Three words can explain both why it's empty and why I chug my beer and get out quickly on this lonely Friday night where the heatwave has finally broken, but it's still in the upper 80's: *broken air conditioner.*

12:15 A.M. Von?

"SATURDAY"

ZAGAT'S LIKE ME

12:05 P.M. Why oh why did I pick the number 99? Fifty would've been good enough. Fifty beers in 50 bars in five days. How many people have gone to 50 bars in five days? I'd be willing to bet not too many, if I was a gambling man, which I'm not. Nor do I ramble, but that's another tale, one perhaps best left for Dickie Betts, or better yet, Bob Seger to explain. But 50 beers, that would've been a big enough deal. I'd have been done two days ago. I would've had three days of my vacation left to lounge around before I had to go back to my horrible, rotten, stinking night job. But no, oh no, I had to be a big shot, to quote Billy Joel, which I really hate to do. I mean, who wants to quote a bald man who's beyond middle age and yet still clings to the childish name of Billy like a security blanket from his lost youth. Billy. . .Billy, Billy, *Billy.* Time for your piano lesson, *Billy.* Look both ways before you cross the street, *Billy*. Don't forget to take your Rogaine, *Billy*. Well, you get the point. I'm beginning to ramble after I pointedly told you I didn't, so let's just forget about Billy and get back to the 99 number.

"Yeah, I can go to 99 bars, no sweat," I casually told all my friends. Well, contrary to my confident yet what now appears to be stupid and rather bold statement, there's been a *lot* of sweat. And mountains upon mountains of other bullshit as well. I've endured crap from cabbies, cripples, frigid psychics, sock vendors, born again Christian women refusing to show me their silver-dollar nipples, psychotic fast-food countermen and an unbearable heatwave that's overworked my sweat glands and sapped me of my energy. And the Marriott bar doesn't spin anymore! It doesn't spin! Motherfucker!!

Goddamn it, I don't know if I can go on. I've got a fucking skull-splitting headache, I'm not sure if I'm capable of swallowing another mouthful of beer, I haven't shaved in seven days, my jeans smell like they've been marinated in sweat and putrid backwash from a case of Budweiser long neck bottles and I've still got a rash on my ass. Yeah, that's right, a rash on my ass. I know you don't want to read about it anymore, but *I'm* the one with the ass rash, not *you*. I've suffered pain you weaklings couldn't even dream about in your most horrific of nightmares, just so all of you sons of bitches could have a fun and wacky little guidebook and travelogue to read. Well, you know what? Fuck this, I'm going back to bed. I quit. What's that? You don't like it? Well go stick a cob up your ass and take the long, low road to hell in a fucking rotten handbasket for all I care. I've had enough. Fuck it.

12:45 P.M. Goddamn it. I can't sleep. I've had four Advil and my head is still pounding like 10 chain gangs on overtime. Aw, screw it. I've gone this far, I might as well finish, I've only got 13 more to go. May as well lay this thing to rest in a proper manner.

I am a professional after all and I *must* keep reminding myself of this. I am a professional. I am a rock. I am an island. And a rock feels no pain. And an island never cries. And a professional can drink 99 beers in seven days. Where in holy hell is Art

Garfunkel when I need him? Art. . .oh, Art? Billy? Billy. . .Billy, Billy, *Billy*.

AUTHOR'S NOTE: *In this chapter all the surveyor's comments will be put in quotes, just like they do in the* Zagat's *guidebooks. Yeah, I know I'm the only surveyor, but humor me, it is the seventh day and all.*

FANELI'S CAFE

94 PRINCE ST. @ MERCER ST.

212.431.5744

BEER - BUDWEISER, $3.50

This place is "fucking packed." I "don't know why." It's pretty much your "ordinary bar" with "tables off to the side joint." I don't "mind the crowd" as much as I "see a lot of assholes in here." The jerkoff "standing next to me" looks like "Ron Mael from the band Sparks." You remember him, "don't you?" He was the one who "played keyboards" and looked like "a cross between a tall Charlie Chaplin and a tall Adolf Hitler." Well, this guy "looks like an evil twin of Ron Mael's," and to top it all off he's wearing this goofy little gray "fedora kind of a hat." Like I said, there's "a lot of assholes in here."

2:20 P.M. You're probably already a little sick of the quotation marks, and it's only been one review. Well, tough luck, Agnes, I'm sick of beer and bars, so welcome to the club. Suck it up. Or should I say, "Suck it up"? Hah!

BAR 89

89 MERCER ST. BETWEEN BROOME AND SPRING STS.

212.274.0989

BEER - HEINEKEN, $5.50

This two-story "bar/restaurant" is done up in "black, white and surgical silver decor." The "sterile atmosphere" makes one feel like "they're at some high-priced doctor's office waiting for a $5,000 rectal exam." What a "fucking snobatorium." The place is just "crawling with rich yuppie scumsuckers" and "pretentious Soho hipsters." I'm the "only person in here" who "looks like a wino that just crawled out of a gutter" after "an eight-day bender." The bartender has "ignored me for five minutes now." I finally "get his attention" by yelling out, "Do you think I can get a drink down here before nightfall?" He serves me my beer with "his nose pointed upward" and I'm "amused at how his nostrils resemble a two-car garage" from this "unique vantage point." What a "fucking dick."

2:50 P.M. I could've picked 60. Twelve beers in twelve bars every day for five days. I could've even managed 65 easily. That's. . .umm. . .it's. . .God, I wish I had a calculator. . .uhh. . . well, it's not 99, that's for sure.

Puck Fair

298 Lafayette St. @ E. Houston St.

212.431.1200

Beer - Red Stripe, $5.00

This "large, high-ceilinged, airy bar" seems even larger since "I'm the only customer here." I try to "chat up the bartender," but he's "having none of it" and walks away to "clean the counter." I'm "all alone." I'm "scared." I "want my mommy." "Help!"

3:22 P.M. As I walk up Broadway in the direction of the next bar, I pass the building where I was first published here in New York. The address is 611 Broadway and the newspaper was a weekly called *NY Weekly*. That first piece I wrote for them is probably my all-time favorite freelance clipping, and here's why.

When I moved here in 1993, the first thing I did was to send portfolios of my writing clips to editors at magazines and newspapers all over town. After sending out dozens of them, I was met with a thundering silence from the publishing world here in Manhattan. Finally, I got a response about four weeks later, at the end of September, a call from the editor of *NY Weekly*. The paper was a thin, fairly new newspaper in the dog eat dog world of this city's weekly newspapers. I forget the editor's name, but it was a woman who told me she was impressed with my writing and would like me to do some feature writing for the paper. I was thrilled; finally someone saw my potential and was going to give me a chance. But as always, there was a catch. She said she was in a bind. She had assigned a writer to a piece and at the last minute

THIS WAS ONE OF THE LEAST SUCCESSFUL BUILDINGS EVER DESIGNED BY SANFORD WHITE. PERHAPS IT WAS BUILT AFTER HE WAS SHOT TO DEATH. I KNOW THAT MY BANK ACCOUNT WAS SHOT TO DEATH AFTER I WORKED THERE FOR AWHILE.

the writer had backed out. And she needed this piece by the next afternoon. Eager to show her I could meet an impossible deadline, I boldly told her, "Whatever it is, you can count on me."

"Oh, great," she replied. "You have done movie reviews, haven't you?" she added.

"I've done hundreds of them," I laughingly spit back. "I did freelance movie reviews for all the papers in Peoria before I moved here."

Of course I had never written a movie review in my life. In fact I hadn't been inside of a movie theater for years, but I figured what the hell? How hard could it be? You watch the movie, you either like it or not and that's the end of the story. The editor was thrilled and said my name would be on a press list at some cineplex in midtown and I could bring a friend if I wanted. The screening was to be at 6 p.m. The movie was called *Judgment Night*.

So I made my way to the theater, but I was early. I asked a ticket seller where I should go to get my pass and she pointed me to a table in the lobby. I walked over, told some dorky kid my name and I was presented with two exclusive press pass tickets and a sheath of papers including a synopsis of the movie, an entire credit list and a complete soundtrack listing. As I scanned the movie credits my stomach sank as I read the three words that can strike mortal fear into the heart of any moviegoer: *Starring Emilio Estevez.* As I read further I realized this was one of those action-teen flicks and I really didn't feel like sitting through it.

I went outside and smoked a cigarette and observed a young couple trying to figure out which movie to go to. That's when an idea hit me and like so many times in my life I acted on this idea without thinking five minutes down the road. What I did was walk over with my press pass tickets and tell them I wasn't going to be able to use them, I had a late breaking story I had to cover and would they like to see a special screening of *Judgment Night?* Naturally they were all impressed with the offer and the guy actually pulled out a twenty and shoved it into my hand after taking the tickets. Of course a journalist knows he should never take any money when writing a story, but since I was doing a movie review, I gladly took the dough, pointed the two in the right direction and hightailed it to the closest bar.

I started constructing my "review" in the bar from the press kit. It pretty much detailed the movie and I built my review around that. I panned the movie, but it also starred Denis Leary, who I think is great, so I gave him a good notice in the review. When I finished the review I felt pretty good about it. It actually read like I sat through the movie. And that's when I decided to push it just a hair further. As I scanned the movie credits, I saw the credit for the "Best Boy." I always wondered what the "Best Boy" on a movie set did. It always sounded like some porno thing to me. So I included a mention of the Best Boy in the review and while thinking it probably wouldn't blow my cover, it would surely be edited out. So imagine my surprise after I turn my review in, and then the following week I pick up the *NY Weekly* and read the following review:

WRONG TURN

By Marty Wombacher
Judgment Night
Starring Emilio Estevez and Denis Leary

Set in Chicago, *Judgment Night* is a tale of a "boys night out" gone frighteningly wrong. Married man Estevez goes out with his unhitched pals and younger brother to a boxing match in the Windy City. En route, they take a wrong expressway ramp and wind up in a neighborhood that's crawling with winos, gangs and violence. While trying to come out alive, they crash their van and witness Denis Leary killing a kid execution-style while his henchmen stand by.

What follows is one long chase scene between bad boy Leary and his brood chasing after Emilio's pack.

While there are some exciting moments in the movie, they seem to be there almost by accident. Another incidental saving grace is former MTV pitchman and comedian Denis Leary. His character is basically an extension of his crazed standup act, but he pushes it to a delightfully manic "Jack Nicholson on crack" persona.

The movie *Judgment Night* may not forge any new territory, but the soundtrack does. It pairs rockers with rappers inventively—Slayer with Ice-T and Faith No More with Boo-Yaa T.R.I.B.E.

Movie afficionados will also recognize legendary Best Boy Bobby Neville in the film's closing credits. Small consolation.

I couldn't believe it, those idiots printed my fake review, word for word, *including* the Best Boy line. Unfuckingbelievable. Of course they got the last laugh. Eight months later the paper went bankrupt owing me well over $600 for features I wrote for them after that review. And my illustrious freelance writing career has spun sideways ever since.

FLANNERY'S BAR

205 W. 14TH ST. BETWEEN 7TH AND 8TH AVES.

212.929.9589

BEER - BUDWEISER, $4.00

Another day, another "fucking Irish bar." Same "green walls," same "long wooden bar," same "Irish bartender," same "drunken hooligans" quaffing down pint after pint of Guinness. I've reviewed "so many" Irish bars this week, there's just "nothing left to say." I'm all "Irished out."

4:35 P.M. As I leave Flannery's for pastures that are any color other than green, I spy a different sort of pub located right next door. It's a small little hole in the wall called the Donut Pub. And it's called the Donut Pub for a very good reason: This place is just jam-packed with donuts. There's coconut cream donuts, Boston cream donuts, marble glazed donuts, jelly donuts, sugar donuts, blueberry donuts, glazed apple donuts, chocolate iced donuts, and in addition there's also a large variety of crullers to be had here. Apple crumb crullers, blueberry crullers, jelly roll crullers, sugar crullers, cinnamon crullers and plain crumb crullers. That's an awful lot of crullers, huh? As I try to decide on what I want to order, the radio in this den of donuts, which is tuned to Lite 106.7, begins to play "Faithfully" by Journey. God, how I hate that song. It's so corny and sickening and barf-inducing. And what about that video that came out to accompany it?

Remember that stinking piece of shit that showed Steve Perry getting all teary-eyed as he shaved off his moustache? Barf, barf and barf. Barfsicle. Barf Simpson. Barf of ages. Barf the magic dragon. Bob Barfer. You know what song I like? "OK Hieronymous" by Graham Parker off his album *The Mona Lisa's Sister*. In addition to just being a great song with original lyrics, it's probably the only pop song in history to refer to Dutch painter Hieronymous Bosch. Bosch's paintings have been likened to grotesque fantasies which show the artist's vision of worldly sin and its eternal damnation.

I wisely decide on a vanilla iced donut because I have to admit that I don't have the faintest idea what a cruller is.

Chicago B.L.U.E.S.

73 8th Ave. between 13th and 14th Sts.

212.924.9755

Beer - Budweiser, $5.00

(Da duh, duh duh) This bar "is dark." *(Da duh, duh duh)* I wish the "drunken couple" who are making out in a "most sloppy manner" would "take it to a hotel already." *(Da duh, duh duh)* Lenny Kravitz's cover of "American Woman" is blaring out of the speakers in the bar. *(Da duh, duh duh)* Golly, I didn't realize Lenny Kravitz "was a bluesman." *(Da duh, duh duh)* I think I'll "leave" before they start in with "the Limp Bizkit." *(Da duh, duh duh, harmonica solo, fade out)*

5:20 P.M. You know what I'm thinking about as I head toward the next bar? The snack cracker Chicken in a Biscuit. I've always enjoyed this tasty snack cracker (and it's doubly good when you spray a large dollop of Easy Cheese on top. If I was a girl I could get away with writing "Yummy!" right now, but sadly I'm a 43-year-old man so I'll just have to say that it's "very, very good!") but I've always wondered about the name, Chicken in a Biscuit. That name brings up some pretty weird mental imagery. You're either going to need an extremely large biscuit or a teeny tiny little chicken to make the thing work, if you really wanted to put a chicken inside of a biscuit that is. Which is what the name implies. And the weird thing is, Chicken in a Biscuit are crackers. They're not biscuits at all. And they really don't taste all that much like chicken. They're just really salty. It's a very strange name for a very strange snack item, but I stand firm in my recommendation for the aforementioned snack item. Thank you for the aintree iron.

HOGS & HEIFERS

859 WASHINGTON ST. @ W. 13TH ST.

PHONE: 212.929.0655

BEER - BUDWEISER, $3.00

Look, by now you know "I'm tired" and "these reviews" are getting "more bitter" by the minute, but this place really "sucks butt cheek." There's nothing more irritating than people who live in a large metropolitan city trying to act like "shit-kicking rednecks." And this place is "devoted to this most sickening strain of humanity." It's all done up in unfinished wood, there's piles of bras thrown by the "drunken sluts" in here who pretend to be

"good ol' gals" looking to pick up one of the "beer- and shot-drinking good ol' boys" in "this dump." And the bartenders in this sewer are "the most annoying people in this galaxy." The female bartenders here wear "leather bras," tight jeans and are full of "fake attitude." Every "five minutes" one will pick up a megaphone and bark at the "sorry-ass losers" in this joint to "make some noise cause this is Hogs and motherfucking Heifers you motherfucking sons of bitches!" Do you "kiss your mother" with that mouth, "sweetie?" I "moved to New York" to get away from this "kind of shit." Oh, and a note to the "good ol' boy" with the ten-gallon hat "drinking shots" at the bar. Hoss never used a cell phone.

6:05 P.M. As I walk to the next bar I'm eating a sandwich I bought at a deli a few minutes ago. It's a ham and cheese hero with mustard. What I'd give to be able to write that it's yummy, because it is, but as you all know by now, I can't. It's very, very good. What an ironic moment, huh? Huh?

THE VILLAGE IDIOT

355 W. 14TH ST. BETWEEN 8TH AND 9TH AVES.

212.989.7334

BEER - BUDWEISER, $3.00

This is "pretty much the same bar as Hogs & Heifers" only the people here "genuinely seem to be retarded." And I'm not making "fun of the retarded" or stooping to a "cheap joke," it's just that all the people here "really seem to be retarded." Really, I'm not joking. And they sell "cans of Pabst Blue Ribbon here." I bet they "sell a lot of them, too." It's tempting to write that "this shithole lives up to its name," and, well, I just wrote it, so there. "Yeeha and woohoo."

6:45 P.M. I haven't mentioned this yet, but I ran out of clean shirts today and I'm wearing the same shirt that I had on last Sunday. As tonight's sweat mingles with last Sunday's dried up sweat. . .I'm not sure what to write here, the fun is draining fast. I'm tired. Very, very tired. And I smell. And I need a shave.

THE RED LIGHT BISTRO

50 9TH AVE. @ 15TH ST.

212.675.2400

BEER - BUDWEISER, $4.00

Contrary to the name, there's "no whores in here."

7:20 P.M. And I'm so sick of beer.

THE GIRL FROM IPANEMA

252 W. 14TH ST. BETWEEN 7TH & 8TH AVES.

212.807.0150

BEER - BUDWEISER, $3.00

This bar is very popular with the "Latino crowd." In fact, I'm the "only white guy in here." A lot of people are "staring at me." And a lot of these people are "men who are bigger than me" and look like they "want to beat the living shit out of me." I feel like an "alcoholic Beaver Cleaver" who's wandered onto the "wrong side of the tracks." I "chug my beer" and thankfully leave with "all of my teeth intact."

8:10 P.M. And I've been drunk for seven nights in a row now.

McKENNA'S PUB

245 W. 14TH ST. @ 7TH AVE.

212.620.8124

BEER - BUDWEISER, $3.50

"Fuck the Irish."

8:45 P.M. And I can't wait for this to be over.

GASLIGHT LOUNGE

400 W. 14TH ST. @ 9TH AVE.

212.807.8444

BEER - BUDWEISER, $4.00

With all the "comfy couches" and "overstuffed chairs" in this large lounge, it gives one "the feeling of drinking in Orson Welles's" den. And who the hell wants "to drink in Orson Welles's den?" "Not me," for starters.

9:15 P.M. And I wonder where that little sock man is tonight?

ANOTHEROOM

249 W. BROADWAY @ N. MOORE ST.

212.226.1418

BEER - BUDWEISER, $3.50

Another "bar," Anotheroom. They're "all the same." A "bar," filled with a "bunch of assholes," "booze". . . "fuck it." "One more to go."

10:15 P.M. He sold all kinds of socks. White socks, dark socks, women's socks, men's socks, plaid socks, striped socks, polka dot socks, ribbed socks, thin socks, thick socks, woolen socks.

No Moore

234 W. Broadway @ N. Moore St.

212.925.2595

"What an aptly titled bar, huh?"

12:15 A.M. Von?

AFTERWORD

S o there you have it. One man's guide to 99 bars in New York City. I'm sure I knocked off a couple of years of my life while writing and researching this, but I learned some valuable lessons along the way. The biggest lesson I learned is about drinking excessive amounts of beer. I've decided to grow up a little and realize that one can't abuse beer every night of his life and still be a productive and professional writer, journalist and human being. Yes, that's right, I've decided to switch to vodka.

Cheers.

HOOD BY HOOD

BARS IN DECLINE

ALHPABETICAL

HOOD BY HOOD

WHERE IT'S AT
TWO TURNTABLES AND
A MICROPHONE

UPPER WEST SIDE

DRIP
489 Amsterdam Ave. bet. 83rd
& 84th Sts.
P&G TAVERN
279 Amsterdam Ave.
@ 73rd St.
ERNIE'S
2150 Broadway bet. 75th &
76th Sts.
PETER'S
182 Columbus Ave. bet. 68th &
69th Sts.

LOWER EAST SIDE

BLARNEY COVE
510 E. 14th St. bet. Aves. A & B
BIG BAR
75 E. 7th St. bet. 1st &
2nd Aves.
ONE AND ONE
76 E. 1st St. @ 1st Ave
THE COCK
188 Ave. A @ 12th St.

CHELSEA

COFFEE SHOP BAR
29 Union Square W. @ 16th St.

LIVE BAIT
14 E. 23rd St. bet. Broadway &
Madison Aves.

OLIVES (AT W HOTEL)
201 Park Ave. S.

119 BAR
119 E. 15th St. bet. Irving Pl. &
Union Square E.

HEARTLAND BREWERY
35 Union Square W. bet. 15th &
16th Sts.

OLD TOWN BAR
45 E. 18th St. bet. Park Ave. &
Broadway

THE TOMATO
676 6th Ave. @ 21st St.

SPAIN
113 W. 13th St. @ 6th Ave.

STONED CROW
85 Washington Pl. bet. 6th Ave.
& Washington Sq. Park

PARK AVALON
225 Park Ave. S. bet. 18th
& 19th Sts.

DUKES
99 East 19th St. @ Lexington
Ave.

PETE'S TAVERN
129 E. 18th St. @ Irving Pl.

COMOLLO'S
359 6th Ave. @ Washington Pl.

FLANNERY'S BAR
205 W. 14th St. bet. 7th &
8th Aves.

MCKENNA'S PUB
245 W. 14th St. @ 7th Ave.

GREENWICH VILLAGE

WHITE HORSE TAVERN
567 Hudson St. @ 11th St.

CALIENTE CAB CO.
61 7th Ave. S. @ Bleecker St.

COWGIRL HALL OF FAME
519 Hudson St. @ 10th St.

CBGB'S 313 GALLERY
313 Bowery @ Bleecker St.

VON
3 Bleecker St. bet. Bowery &
Layfayette St.

BLEECKER STREET BAR
58 Bleecker St. @ Crosby St.

SEÑOR SWANKY'S
142 Bleecker St. @ LaGuardia
Pl.

LA MARGARITA
184 Thompson St. @ Bleecker
St.

PECULIER PUB
145 Bleecker St. bet. LaGuardia
Pl. & Thompson St.

THE BITTER END
147 Bleecker St. bet. LaGuardia
Pl. & Thompson St.

KENNY'S CASTAWAYS
157 Bleecker St. bet. Thompson
& Sullivan Sts.

THE BACK FENCE
155 Bleecker St. @
Thompson St.

VILLAGE LANTERN
167 Bleecker St. @ Sullivan St.

ARTHUR'S TAVERN
57 Grove St. bet. Bleecker St. &
7th Ave.

JEKYLL & HYDE
91 7th Ave. S. bet. Bleecker &
Christopher Sts.

UPPER EAST SIDE

JACKSON HOLE
1611 2nd Ave. bet. 83rd & 84th
Sts.

RATHBONES
1702 2nd Ave. @ 88th St.

MARTY O'BRIEN'S
1696 2nd Ave. bet 87th &
88th Sts.

ELAINE'S
1703 2nd Ave. bet. 88th & 89th
Sts.

HEADLINES
1678 1st Ave. bet 87th & 88th
Sts.

WHO'S ON FIRST
1683 1st Ave. @ 87th St.

IGGY'S KICK ASS BAR
1452 2nd Ave. @ 76th St.

FLIGHT 1668
1668 3rd Ave. bet. 93rd & 94th
Sts.

**BARCOASTAL (FORMERLY THE
COWBOY BAR)**
1495 1st Ave. @ 78th St.

MIDTOWN

**BLARNEY STONE (THREE
LOCATIONS)**
106 W. 32nd St. bet. 6th & 7th
Aves.
410 8th Ave. bet. 30th & 31st
Sts.
340 9th Ave. bet. 29th &
30th Sts.

EAMONN DORAN
136 W. 33rd St. @ 6th Ave.

THE IRISH PUB
837 7th Ave. @ 54th St.

LUNDY BROS.
205 W. 50th St. bet. 7th Ave. &
Broadway

MARTINI'S BAR
810 7th Ave. @ 53rd St.

SHERATON HOTEL BAR
811 7th Ave. @ 52nd St.

**HUDSON'S SPORTS BAR (IN
THE SHERATON HOTEL)**
811 7th Ave. @ 52nd St.

MANHATTAN CHILI CO.
1697 Broadway @ 53rd St.

BEEKMAN BAR AND BOOKS
889 1st Ave. @ 50th St.

HOWARD JOHNSON'S
1551 Broadway @ 46th St.

THE MARRIOTT HOTEL BAR
1535 Broadway @ 45th St.

THE HARD ROCK CAFE
221 W. 57th St. bet. 7th Ave.
& Broadway

HARLEY DAVIDSON CAFE
1370 6th Ave. @ 56th St.

HOOTERS
211 W. 56th St. bet. Broadway
& 7th Ave.

ESPN ZONE
1472 Broadway @ 42nd St.

PIG 'N' WHISTLE
165 W. 47th St. bet 6th &
7th Aves.

**BRIDGES BAR (IN THE
HILTON HOTEL)**
1335 6th Ave. @ 54th St.

OLD CASTLE PUB
160 W. 54th St. @ 7th Ave.

THE OAK ROOM
768 5th Ave. @ 59th St.

**WWF (WORLD WRESTLING
FEDERATION) NEW YORK**
1501 Broadway
@ 43rd St.

LANGAN'S
150 W. 47th St. @ 7th Ave.

**TWIST (IN THE AMERITANIA
HOTEL)**
230 W. 54th St. @ Broadway

KENNEDY'S
327 W. 57th St. bet. 8th & 9th Aves.

JIMMY WALKER'S ALE HOUSE
245 E. 55th St. bet. 2nd & 3rd Aves.

MUSTANG SALLY'S
324 7th Ave. bet. 28th & 29th Sts.

MUSTANG HARRY'S
352 7th Ave. bet 29th & 30th Sts.

53RD ST. CIGAR BAR
811 7th Ave. @ 53rd St.

COOPER'S CIGAR BAR
41 W. 58th St. bet 5th & 6th Aves.

BILL'S GAY NINETIES
57 E. 54th St. bet. Madison & Park Aves.

SOHO

VG BAR
643 Broadway @ Bleecker St.

FANELI'S CAFE
94 Prince St. @ Mercer St.

BAR 89
89 Mercer St. bet. Broome & Spring Sts.

PUCK FAIR
298 Lafayette St. @ E. Houston St.

HELL'S KITCHEN

SMITHS
701 8th Ave. @ 44th St.

COLLINS
735 8th Ave. bet 46th & 47th Sts.

THESE BARS ARE ON THE CUSP OF DIFFERENT NEIGHBORHOODS,

So You Figure It Out, We've Got Better Things to Do

PADDY MAGUIRE'S
237 3rd Ave. @ 21st St.

McCARTHEY'S
345 2nd Ave. @ 20th St.

McSWIGGANS
393 2nd Ave. @ 20th St.

McCORMACKS
365 3rd Ave. bet. 26th & 27th Sts.

PADDY REILLY'S
519 2nd Ave. @ 29th St.

BONGO
299 10th Ave. bet. 27th & 28th Sts.

FLIGHT 151
151 8th Ave. bet. 17th & 18th Sts.

CHICAGO B.L.U.E.S.
73 8th Ave. bet. 13th & 14th Sts.

HOGS & HEIFERS
859 Washington St. @ W. 13th St.

THE RED LIGHT BISTRO
50 9th Ave. @ 15th St.

THE GIRL FROM IPANEMA
252 W. 14th St. bet. 7th & 8th Aves.

GASLIGHT LOUNGE
400 W. 14th St. @ 9th Ave.

ANOTHEROOM
249 W. Broadway @ N. Moore St.

NO MOORE
234 W. Broadway @ N. Moore St.

99 IN DECLINE INDEX

THE BEST, THE REST, AND THE WORST

1   (The Best) P&G Tavern
2   Stoned Crow (Actually this ties with the best because it's the author's neighborhood bar and maybe he'll get a free drink out of this deal.)
3   Old Town Bar
4   Iggy's Kick Ass Bar
5   Big Bar
6   One and One
7   Kennedy's
8   119 Bar
9   Langan's
10 Dukes
11 White Horse Tavern
12 Peculier Pub
13 No Moore
14 Beekman Bar and Books
15 Pig 'n' Whistle
16 Flight 151
17 Flight 1668
18 Kenny's Castaways
19 The Back Fence
20 Ernie's
21 Bongo
22 Drip
23 CBGB's 313 Gallery
24 Collins
25 Howard Johnson's
26 Bleecker Street Bar
27 The Oak Room

28   Jimmy Walker's Ale House
29   Pete's Tavern
30   Puck Fair
31   Arthur's Tavern
32   Village Lantern
33   Anotheroom
34   Martini's Bar
35   The Red Light Bistro
36   Spain
37   Rathbones
38   Live Bait
39   Bridges Bar (In the Hilton Hotel)
40   McCarthey's
41   Paddy Maguire's
42   La Margarita
43   Sheraton Hotel Bar
44   Faneli's Cafe
45   The Cock
46   McSwiggans
47   Twist (in the Ameritania Hotel)
48   Paddy Reilly's
49   Blarney Rock
50   Chicago B.L.U.E.S.
51   Marty O'Brien's
52   Mustang Sally's
53   Mustang Harry's
54   McCormacks
55   Bill's Gay Nineties
56   Von
57   Blarney Stone
58   Blarney Stone
59   Blarney Stone
60   VG Bar
61   Olives (At W Hotel)
62   The Tomato
63   Who's on First
64   Caliente Cab Co.
65   Hooters

66   Manhattan Chili Co.
67   Cowgirl Hall of Fame
68   The Irish Pub
69   Barcoastal (formerly the Cowboy Bar)
70   Señor Swanky's
71   The Marriott Hotel Bar
72   Flannery's Bar
73   Smiths
74   Coffee Shop Bar
75   The Hard Rock Cafe
76   Harley Davidson Cafe
77   Jekyll & Hyde
78   Blarney Cove
79   Eamonn Doran
80   Hudson's Sports Bar (in the Sheraton Hotel)
81   Old Castle Pub
82   Comollo's
83   McKenna's Pub
84   Gaslight Lounge
85   Headlines
86   The Girl From Ipanema
87   Cooper's Cigar Bar
88   53rd Street Cigar Bar
89   The Bitter End
90   Jackson Hole
91   Elaine's
92   Heartland Brewery
93   ESPN Zone
94   WWF (World Wrestling Federation)
95   Park Avalon
96   Peter's
97   Bar 89 (Real Close to the Worst)
98   Village Idiot (Even Closer to the Worst)
99   Hogs & Heifers (The Worst)

IN DECLINE

ALPHABETICAL INDEX

A

Anotheroom, 161
Arthur's Tavern, 144

B

The Back Fence, 143
Bar 89, 150
Barcoastal (formerly the Cowboy Bar), 122
Beekman Bar and Books, 47
Big Bar, 56
Bill's Gay Nineties, 124
The Bitter End, 140
Blarney Cove, 23
Blarney Rock, 28
Blarney Stone (three locations), 29
Bleecker Street Bar, 135

Bongo, 55
Bridges Bar (In the Hilton Hotel), 72

C

Caliente Cab Co., 84
CBGB's 313 Gallery, 133
Chicago B.L.U.E.S., 156
The Cock, 125
Coffee Shop Bar, 40
Collins, 91
Comollo's, 146
Cooper's Cigar Bar, 113
Cowgirl Hall of Fame, 122

D

Dukes, 101
Drip, 43

E

Eamonn Doran, 32
Elaine's, 78
Ernie's, 45
ESPN Zone, 69

F

Faneli's Cafe, 149
53rd St. Cigar Bar, 112
Flannery's Bar, 155
Flight 151, 120
Flight 1668, 121

G

Gaslight Lounge, 161
The Girl From Ipanema, 160

H

The Hard Rock Cafe, 52
Harley Davidson Cafe, 53
Headlines, 96
Heartland Brewery, 63
Hogs & Heifers, 157
Hooters, 53
Howard Johnson's, 49
Hudson's Sports Bar (in the Sheraton Hotel), 37

I

Iggy's Kick Ass Bar, 102
The Irish Pub, 35

J

Jackson Hole, 47
Jekyll & Hyde, 145
Jimmy Walker's Ale House, 96

K

Kennedy's, 94
Kenny's Castaways, 141

L

La Margarita, 137
Langan's, 86
Live Bait, 55

M

Manhattan Chili Co., 38
The Marriott Hotel Bar, 50
Martini's Bar, 36
Marty O'Brien's, 77
McCarthey's, 24
McCormacks, 26
McKenna's Pub, 160
McSwiggans, 25
Mustang Harry's, 105
Mustang Sally's, 104

N

No Moore, 162

O

The Oak Room, 75
Old Castle Pub, 74
Old Town Bar, 66
Olives (At W Hotel), 56
119 Bar, 62
One and One, 61

P

P&G Tavern, 44
Paddy Maguire's, 21
Paddy Reilly's, 27
Park Avalon, 98
Peculier Pub, 138
Peter's, 108
Pete's Tavern, 107
Puck Fair, 151

Q

Sadly, we didn't visit any "Q" bars.

ALPHABETICAL

R

Rathbones, 76
Red Light Bistro, 159

S

Señor Swanky's, 136
Sheraton Hotel Bar , 37
Smiths, 88
Spain, 82
Stoned Crow, 97

T

The Tomato, 68
Twist (in the Ameritania Hotel), 87

U

See, "Q."

V

Village Idiot, 158
VG Bar, 135

Village Lantern, 144
Von, 134

W

White Horse Tavern, 54
Who's on First, 97
WWF (World Wrestling
    Federation), 85

X

See, "U."

Y

See, "X."

Z

See, "Y."

ALPHABETICAL

ABOUT EDWARD HOPPER

NOT A HOPPER.

Edward Hopper was born in 1882. While Hopper was first recognized in the art world for his etchings, he later returned to painting. His works were often large, quiet urban studies that revealed a subtle sense of composition that mirrored his feelings of loneliness and alienation.

Hopper died in 1967, the same year that "Love Is Only Sleeping" by the Monkees was released on the album *Pisces, Aquarius, Capricorn & Jones Ltd.*

Contrary to (some) public opinion, the Monkees played instruments on a lot of their tunes, including this one featuring Michael Nesmith on lead vocal and guitar; Mickey Dolenz, background vocals; Peter Tork, keyboards; and Davy Jones, percussion. The session players on this song were Chip Douglas, bass; Eddie Hoh, drums; and Bill Chadwick, sound effects. Chip Douglas produced the song, it was written by Barry Mann and Cynthia Weil and while it was originally slated to be a single, it never came to pass.

ABOUT THE AUTHOR

Photo © 2001 by Frank Scott

Marty Wombacher is the editor and writer of *fishwrap* magazine. In addition, he's written for *Time Out New York*, *Gadfly*, *Curio*, *Nerve*, ny.citysearch.com, and he writes a column that encompasses gardening, wart removal and other humorous facets of everyday life for *Toast* magazine, at www.toastmag.com.

   He resides in Manhattan with his two pet plastic alligators, Gomer and Sgt. Carter. Mr. Wombacher believes that Joan Jett is God and his socks are often mismatched. He's listening to "Love Is Only Sleeping" by the Monkees as he writes this. Yabba, dabba and, of course, do. "Wilma!!!"